# OPEN ROAD'S
# BEST OF ARIZONA

### 5th Revised Edition

## by Becky Youman

*Open Road Travel Guides – designed for the amount of time you really have for your trip!*

# Open Road Publishing

*Open Road's Best of Arizona*
*5th Edition*

To my traveling partners – Bryan and Sierra

Text Copyright © 2016 by Becky Youman
- All Rights Reserved -
ISBN 13: 978-1-59360-221-5
Library of Congress Control No. 2016919486

Maps by designmaps.com except Phoenix Light Rail Map, which appears courtesty
of Valley Metro (www.valleymetro.org). The author has made every effort to be as
accurate as possible, but neither she nor the publisher assumes responsibility for the
services provided by any business listed in this guide; for any errors or omissions; or
any loss, damage, or disruptions in your travels for any reason.

## About the Author
Becky Youman first lived in Arizona as a graduate student, where she took advantage
of not having class on Fridays and explored the state every weekend. She moved
back ten years later with her family and has called both Scottsdale and Flagstaff
home for the last decade. She is a freelance writer who has written travel guides
to Chile, Ecuador & the Galapagos Islands, and Mexico. She is also a mom, wife,
mountain biker, surfer, yogini, tequila aficionada, and bookworm.

*For photo credits, please see page 182.*

# TABLE OF CONTENTS

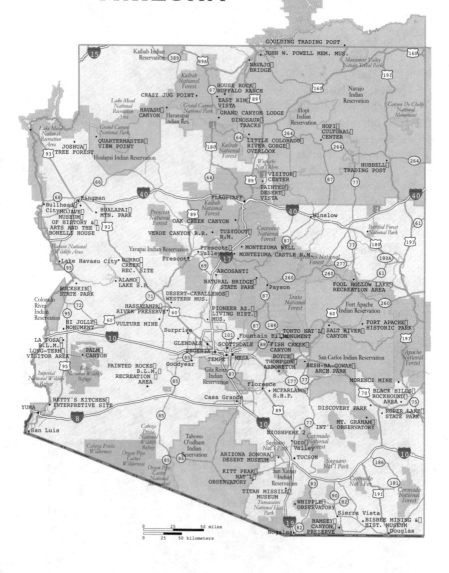

# ARIZONA

GOULDING TRADING POST
JOHN W. POWELL MEM. MUS.
15
Kaibab Indian
Reservation
389
89A
NAVAJO
BRIDGE
Monument Valley
Navajo Tribal Park
160
191
Kaibab
National
Forest
HOUSE ROCK
BUFFALO RANCH
67
EAST RIM
VISTA
89
160
Navajo
Indian
Reservation
Canyon De Chelly
National
Monument
CRAZY JUG POINT
Lake Mead
National
Recreation
Area
HAVASU
CANYON
Grand Canyon
National Park
GRAND CANYON LODGE
DINOSAUR
TRACKS
Hopi
Indian
Reservation
HOPI
CULTURAL
CENTER
264
Lake Mead
National
Recreation
Area
JOSHUA
TREE FOREST
93
Grand Canyon
National Park
Havasupai
Indian Res.
QUARTERMASTER
VIEW POINT
1
64
180
LITTLE COLORADO
RIVER GORGE
OVERLOOK
264
264
HUBBELL
TRADING POST
264
Hualapai Indian Reservation
Kaibab
National
Forest
Wupatki
Nat'l Mon.
66
64
89
VISITOR
CENTER
87
77
68
Kingman
40
FLAGSTAFF
Kaibab
National
Forest
PAINTED
DESERT
VISTA
40
Bullhead
CITY
MOJAVE
MUSEUM
OF HISTORY &
ARTS AND THE
BONELLI HOUSE
HUALAPAI
MTN. PARK
93
Prescott
National
Forest
89
OAK CREEK CANYON
40
Winslow
Coconino
National
Forest
Petrified Forest
National Park
61
VERDE CANYON R.R.
TUZIGOOT
N.M.
87
180
191
Yavapai Indian Reservation
Prescott
Valley
MONTEZUMA WELL
MONTEZUMA CASTLE N.M.
Sitgreaves National
Forest
77
277
180A
Lake Havasu City
95
BURRO
CREEK
REC. SITE
Prescott
17
69
ARCOSANTI
260
260
61
Colorado
River
Indian
Reservation
BUCKSKIN
STATE PARK
72
ALAMO
LAKE S.P.
71
NATURAL
BRIDGE
STATE PARK
Payson
FOOL HOLLOW LAKE
RECREATION AREA
95
HI JOLLY
MONUMENT
60
HASSAYAMPA
RIVER PRESERVE
60
DESERT-CABALLEROS
WESTERN MUS.
87
Tonto
National
Forest
Fort Apache
Indian Reservation
260
LA POSA
B.L.M.
LONG-TERM
VISITOR AREA
VULTURE MINE
PIONEER AZ.
LIVING HIST.
MUS.
60
FORT APACHE
HISTORIC PARK
Surprise
87
188
TONTO NAT'L MONUMENT
SALT RIVER
CANYON
191
95
PALM
CANYON
101
Fountain Hills
SCOTTSDALE
86
FISH CREEK
CANYON
San Carlos Indian Reservation
Apache
National
Forest
Imperial
National Wildlife
Refuge
Kofa
National Wildlife
Refuge
PAINTED ROCKS
B.L.M.
RECREATION
AREA
GLENDALE
85
PHOENIX
Goodyear
TEMPE
MESA
BOYCE
THOMPSON
ARBORETUM
BESH-BA-GOWAH
ARCH. PARK
MORENCI MINE
Gila River
Indian
Reservation
87
77
BLACK HILLS
ROCKHOUND
AREA
70
75
YUMA
8
BETTY'S KITCHEN
INTERPRETIVE SITE
85
Florence
MCFARLAND
S.H.P.
77
Casa Grande
DISCOVERY PARK
ROPER LAKE
STATE PARK
San Luis
Cabeza
Prieta
National
Wildlife
Refuge
85
89
10
MT. GRAHAM
INT'L OBSERVATORY
Cabeza Prieta
Wilderness
Organ Pipe
Cactus
Wilderness
Tahono
O'odham
Indian
Reservation
86
BIOSPHERE 2
Saguaro
Nat'l Park
Oro
Valley
Coronado
National
Forest
Organ Pipe
Cactus
National
Monument
85
ARIZONA SONORA
DESERT MUSEUM
TUCSON
Saguaro
Nat'l Park
186
10
KITT PEAK
NAT'L
OBSERVATORY
San Xavier
Indian
Reservation
181
TITAN MISSILE
MUSEUM
Tumacacori
National Hist.
Park
83
WHIPPLE
OBSERVATORY
90
82
191
Coronado
Nat'l For.
19
RAMSEY
CANYON
PRESERVE
82
Sierra Vista
BISBEE MINING &
HIST. MUSEUM
Nogales
Douglas

0    25    50 miles
0    25    50 kilometers

# 1. INTRODUCTION

**ARIZONA'S** natural wonders – from the vast expanse of the Grand Canyon to the strange and fiery red rocks of Sedona to the surreal forests of fifty foot high Saguaro cactus – are unparalleled in the country. Every part of the state is filled with amazing physical landscapes that showcase nature's offerings. These range from wildflower-dotted deserts to lush alpine forests. Add to that the fascinating influence of both Native American and Hispanic cultures and you've got a destination that is truly unique in terms of scenery, history, architecture, and cuisine.

This book will guide you to the best of the best. Whether you desire a break at one of the world's greatest full-service luxury resorts or prefer a relaxing stay at a historic railroad inn, Arizona's got it and this book will take you there. We offer five-star southwestern cuisine prepared using classic French methods as well as shacks serving up Navajo tacos and fry-bread. You'll get

the run-down on the state's most popular attractions as well others that might not get as much press but are truly worthy of a visit.

This guide covers all the information you need to plan day trips, weekend jaunts, or longer excursions through beautiful Arizona without burdening you with options that simply aren't worth your precious vacation time. Just take off and enjoy – you've got a great trip ahead!

# 2. Overview

Arizona's abundant natural beauty is no secret, but that's only part of the story. The state enjoys a unique ethos that results from a mosaic of cultural influences. Both the Hispanic (in the form of Spanish and Mexican traditions) and the Native American impacts are strong. In fact, almost the entire northeastern quarter of the state is occupied by Indian reservations, especially those of the Navajo and Hopi.

The "Old West" influence survives in Arizona's populace, despite the influx of people from all over the country. In many things, from politics to such mundane issues as Daylight Savings Time, Arizonians forge their own path.

To make planning your trip easier, this book has been divided into seven different touring regions. The remainder of this chapter will briefly describe each of the regions and suggest a few itineraries.

## PHOENIX

The state's capital and largest city, Phoenix is also Arizona's economic, cultural and recreational heart. Centrally located, it is a good spot for reaching out into most parts of the state as well as the logical arrival point for visitors coming in by air.

A modern city with fine museums and numerous cultural attractions, greater Phoenix, also called The Valley, is home to more than a dozen world-class luxury resorts and numerous fine dining establishments. Progressive and vibrant, Phoenix has something for everyone.

## TUCSON

Smaller than Phoenix, Tucson retains a greater Hispanic and Native American presence than its more cosmopolitan sister to the north. That influence, along with the fine museums and University of Arizona, combine to give Tucson a rich cultural life. Luxury resorts abound, as do some of the state's

## Arizona's Best
- **Grand Canyon** – Northwestern Arizona
- **Red Rocks of Sedona** – North-Central Arizona
- **Monument Valley** – Northeastern Arizona
- **Canyon de Chelly** – Northeastern Arizona
- **Sonoran Desert** – Tucson
- **Funky Mining Town of Bisbee** – Southern Arizona
- **Scottsdale Resorts, Night on the Town** – Phoenix

best guest ranches. Day trips south to Mexico and Old West towns like Tombstone and Bisbee are popular diversions for many Tucson visitors.

## NORTH-CENTRAL ARIZONA

Comprised of Sedona, Flagstaff, Prescott, and Jerome, this region is incredibly diverse. Located almost entirely within a series of national forests, it's one of the best areas in the state for outdoor recreation.

Flagstaff is a gateway to the Grand Canyon, as well as a central location for visiting several fascinating national monuments that feature unusual geological phenomena and the remains of ancient civilizations. It's also got some of the most easily accessed snow skiing in the state. Yes, there are pine-covered mountains in Arizona.

The picturesque artist's community of Sedona is home to the famous red rocks of Oak Creek Canyon and numerous recreational opportunities. Prescott and Jerome, with rich histories of cowboys and miners, both hearken back to the days of the Wild West.

## GRAND CANYON

You could take a week in Arizona and visit only the Grand Canyon. You can opt for the easy way and see it from the rim; or be more adventurous and hike or take a mule ride down into the canyon. Or maybe you want to view it from the air or from a raft on the Colorado River. The possibilities are endless and no matter how little or much time you have, the experience will be a rewarding one.

## NORTHEASTERN ARIZONA

The Navajo Indian Reservation is the largest in the United States. It completely surrounds the smaller Hopi Reservation. Together they comprise almost the entire northeastern portion of  Arizona. Many areas are open to the public and you can learn much about the Navajo and Hopi cultures. Scenery and history also abound in this region with outstanding ruins, canyons, and monolithic rock formations.

## EASTERN ARIZONA

This mountainous region, a haven for the desert-dwellers of Phoenix and Tucson, is little known outside the state. You'll find the scenic Mogollon Rim and the beautiful White Mountains, which are perfect for both cool-weather getaways in the summer and snow play in the winter months.

## WESTERN ARIZONA

This area is the least developed, both in population and tourist facilities. Along the western border of the state however (the Colorado River), there are numerous recreation and resort options. There's Lake Havasu, with the original London Bridge, as well as Bullhead City, just across the river from the gambling town of Laughlin, Nevada. Don't forget Kingman, with its Route 66 roots, and Wickenburg, home of numerous dude ranches.

## ITINERARIES

If you've never been to Arizona before, make sure you hit the highlights. If all you've got is a weekend, you should cover both the amazing vistas of the Grand Canyon and the red rocks of Sedona, stopping at the cliff dwellings of Montezuma National Monument on your way back to Phoenix. If you've got a week, you can fit in Sedona, Flagstaff and its surrounding monuments, the Grand Canyon, Canyon de Chelly, and Monument Valley. You will also have time for some R&R in Scottsdale or Tucson.

Each destination chapter of the book points out the best sights in that region, so another option is to just pick out those that sound interesting and make up the perfect itinerary for you.

- Spend Saturday admiring the canyon be it on a hike, bike ride, car or shuttle tour, or helicopter flight. Follow up your fantastic day with a gourmet dinner at the National Park's historic El Tovar Hotel.
- Wake up early Sunday to catch sunrise at the Canyon and then head south to the surreal red rocks formations of Sedona for a late breakfast at the creekside L'Auberge de Sedona. Take a hike, wander through art galleries, or go on an off-road jeep tour, all the while surrounded by stunning sandstone peaks.
- Stop by the impressive 12th-century cliff dwelling at Montezuma Castle National Monument on the way back to the airport in Phoenix.

### Best of Arizona in a Week

- Start your trip in the red rocks of Sedona, where you can enjoy the scenery from a variety of vantage points that range from the seat of a mountain bike to a Jacuzzi at a spa.
- Wind up spectacular Oak Creek Canyon to Flagstaff, where you can enjoy the vibe of this laid-back mountain town. Visit a museum, tour one of the area national monuments, take a hike, or enjoy an event at the local university.
- Next stop – Grand Canyon National Park. Whether you see it from land, air, car, or bike, it will be one of the highlights of your trip. Catch a sunset or sunrise while you are there.
- The Grand Canyon is just one of the impressive sights in northern Arizona. The Navajo Nation and Hopi Reservation are home to some of the most iconic western landscapes. Spend a few days visiting the Monument Valley National Tribal Park, Canyon de Chelly National Monument, and Navajo National Monument.
- Enjoy the last days of your trip with a little time in the city, opting for R&R in either Tucson or Phoenix/Scottsdale. Hit the links, the spa, or a night out on the town.

# 3.Phoenix &
# Scottsdale

**HIGHLIGHTS**
- **The Heard Museum** – amazing Native American culture on display

- **The Desert Botanical Garden** – haunting, fascinating cacti and other desert plants

- **The Musical Instrument Museum** (MIM) – enlightening and foot-tapping exhibits and concerts

- **Old Town Scottsdale** – fine arts and finer nightlife

- Frank Lloyd Wright's legacy at the **Arizona Biltmore** and **Taliesin West**

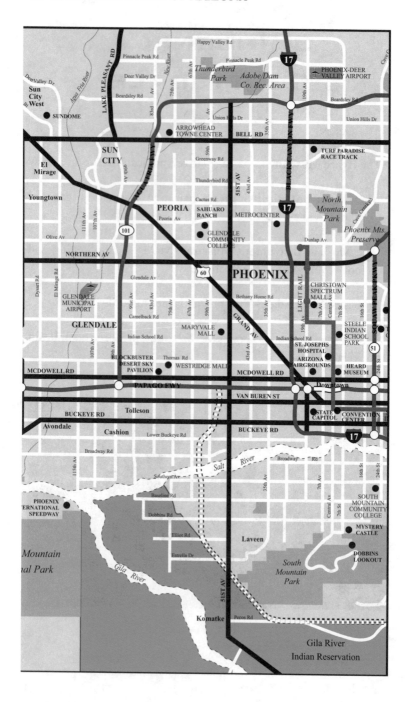

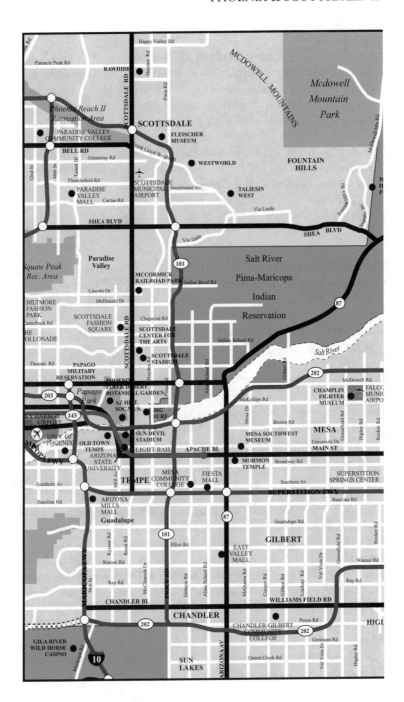

## First Fridays at "RoRo"

**Roosevelt Row Arts District**, nicked named **RoRo**, is downtown Phoenix's hub of art and culture. This increasingly hipster district is especially popular the first Friday of the month when galleries, boutiques, bars, and restaurants are hopping from 6pm-11pm. Regardless of the day, RoRo is worth a visit to witness the revitalization of downtown. Try the **DeSoto Central Market** (*915 N Central Ave*) or **PHX Public Market Café** (*14 E Pierce St.*) for a tasty bite in a cool locale; The **Grand Central Coffee Company** (*718 N Central*) or the **Velo** (*282 N 2nd St.*) for a good cup of joe surrounded by unique décor; or **Hanny's** (*40 N 1st St.*) for a lively good time. *Info: www.rooseveltrow. org.*

**Greater Phoenix**, otherwise known as "The Valley," is a thriving and fast-growing metropolis surrounded by arid mountains and blessed with an average of **300 sunny days a year**. In the heart of the Valley is Phoenix proper, where you'll find many cultural activities, excellent restaurants, and a reinvigorated downtown that is home to a number of professional sports teams.

Just to the east is Scottsdale, the epicenter of the Valley's luxury resorts and golf courses. Museums and restaurants catering to both the well-heeled and the hip abound here. South of Scottsdale is collegiate Tempe, home to the Sun Devils of Arizona State University. Scottsdale, Tempe, Mesa and Chandler are often referred to as the "East Valley." The West Valley includes the city of Glendale, home to the Arizona Cardinals NFL team.

## ORIENTATION

Phoenix is in the Salt River Valley, surrounded by mountains to the east and west. If you're driving into downtown Phoenix from the airport, get onto I-10 and head west for downtown. If you are headed to Scottsdale, go east on the 202 then north on the 101. Phoenix is centrally located, just south of the middle of the state. For **Arrivals & Departures** information for this region, see the *Practical Matters* chapter at the back of the book.

## SEEING THE SIGHTS

### Phoenix

The **Heard Museum**, housed in a gorgeous Spanish Colonial building, offers one of the world's finest collections of southwestern art and culture.

With over 35,000 Native American objects in seven different galleries, the museum simply has more displays than you can take in. **Focus on the HOME: Native People of the Southwest** gallery, an interactive exhibit that chronicles the cultures of America's Indians. Don't miss fascinating displays like a Navajo hogan and Hopi piki room. When buying your tickets ask if there are any **live demonstrations**. The museum often features native artisans discussing their techniques as they work. The **Courtyard Café** is a pleasant spot to grab a bite to eat as well – don't miss the pozole. *Info: 2103 N Central Ave. Light Rail Stop - Central/Encanto/Heard Museum. Tel. 602-252-8848. www.heard.org. Open 9:30am-5pm Monday-Saturday, 11am-5pm Sunday, 6pm-10pm First Fridays (except March). Admission: $18 adults, $7.50 children 6-12.*

After visiting the museum, it's worth taking some time to tour the impeccably restored Tudor, Spanish Revival and Bungalow homes in the adjacent **Willo historic district**. Start by foot or car at 3rd Avenue and McDowell and head north to Thomas and west to 7th Avenue. You can also stop by the expansive Encanto Park at 15 Avenue and Virginia.

Located a few blocks south of the Heard Museum, the **Phoenix Art Museum** offers world-class exhibits in a cool and clean modern space. Palette, located inside, is a pleasant place for a casual lunch. (You don't have to pay to enter the museum if all you're doing is eating lunch.) *Info: 1625 N. Central Avenue. Tel. 602-257-1222. Light Rail Stop - Central/McDowell. www.phxart.org. Open Wednesday 10am-9pm, Thursday-Saturday 10am to 5pm, Sunday 12pm-5pm, 6pm-10pm First Fridays. Admission: $15 adults, $6 children 6-17. Free admission Wednesday 3-9pm.*

Located just down the street from the Phoenix Art Museum, **Burton Barr Central Library** – yes, that's right – the library, merits a visit, especially on a hot day. The futuristic architecture is unique among Phoenix public buildings

### Traveling with Kids?

If you are traveling with kids under 10, they will appreciate a stop at the nearby *Children's Museum of Phoenix*. With hands on, interactive exhibits, like the very popular noodle forest, the museum knows what keeps young ones entertained. *Info: 215 N. 7th Street (SE corner of 7th Street and Van Buren). Tel. 602-253-0501. www.childrensmuseumofphoenix.org. Open Tuesday-Sunday 9am-4pm. Admission: $11.*

and is complemented by state-of-the-art technology inside. Computers run large blinds and sails that open and close to regulate the amount of sunlight coming into the building. *Info: 1221 N. Central Ave. Light Rail Stop - Central/ McDowell. Tel. 602-262-4636. www.phoenixpubliclibrary.org. Open Tuesday-Thursday 9am-9pm, Monday, Friday, Saturday 9am-5pm, and Sunday 1-5pm. Free admission.*

South of the library, on the other side of I-10, you'll find downtown Phoenix's **Heritage Square**. There's not much left of the original Phoenix town site, but eight of the city's residential structures have been restored here. You can tour the Rosson House, a Victorian mansion built by the city's mayor in 1895, for a look at how the Rich & Famous lived back in the day. *Info: 115 N 6$^{th}$ St., Light Rail Stop – Van Buren. Tel. 602-262-5029. Rossonhousemuseum.org. Wednesday-Saturday 10am-4pm. Sunday noon-4pm. Admission: $7.50 adults, $4 children 6-12.* The **Arizona Science Center**, a hit with curious kids, is also located on the grounds. *Info: 600 E. Washington, Light Rail Stop 3$^{rd}$ & Washington. Tel. 602-617-200. www.azscience. org. 10am-5pm daily. Admission: $18 adults, $13 children.*

Eight miles northeast of downtown Phoenix is the iconic **Arizona Biltmore and Villas** (see *Where to Stay*). Influenced by the famous architect **Frank Lloyd Wright** and built in the 1920s, the Arizona Biltmore was the first of the Phoenix area's modern luxury resorts. The Wright style is notable for its harmonious integration of physical structures with natural surroundings, which you'll notice as you approach the complex. Take a walk around the resort to admire the architectural details, many of which are pointed out by plaques. If you want to sit and rest your legs while sipping a cool drink  or enjoying a light meal, there is no better place than under the loggia at **The Café**. From the patio you look out at the colorful gardens framing the perfect mountain vista. Perhaps the biggest draw to Heritage Square, other than numerous festivals, is the renowned **Pizzeria Bianco** (see *Where to Eat*) located in was once the Baird Machine Shop. It's a long wait for a table, but worth it.

You might want to stay and enjoy the view all day, but it will be worth tearing yourself away for a visit to the **Musical Instrument Museum** (**MIM**). The newest museum in Phoenix is also one of its best. Located in north Phoenix relatively near Scottsdale, the MIM has won national accolades for its 20,000 square feet of displays showcasing musical artifacts from all over the world. Guests wear specially designed wireless headsets that play audio clips related to the displays, which are arranged geographically. The **MIM concert hall** is also a great place to catch a wide variety of acts from around the globe. *Info: 4725 E. Mayo Blvd, Phoenix, 85050. Tel. 480-478-6000. www.mim.org. Open Monday-Saturday 9am-5pm and Sunday 10am-5pm. Admission: $18 adults, $10 children 4-12.*

The remarkable **Desert Botanical Garden** is another deservedly popular Phoenix attraction. Spread out over 145 acres, the Botanical Garden has over 20,000 plant specimens representing about 4,000 species native to the world's most arid climates. Head straight to the Desert Discovery Trail, a brick path that winds one-third of a mile through the oldest plantings in the garden. The strange, quiet beauty of these plants that survive the harshest of elements will undoubtedly surprise and intrigue you. (In the summer months you will want to visit the Botanical Garden in the relative cool of the morning and then hit the air-conditioned museums in the heat of the afternoon.) *Info: 2101 N Galvin Parkway in Papago Park. Tel. 480-941-1225. www.dbg.org. Open daily October though April 8am-8pm; May-September 7am-8pm. Admission: $22 adults, $10 children 3-12.*

The Desert Botanical Garden is located right next to the **Phoenix Zoo**, so if you have little ones in tow you might want to take time for a stop at both places.

### Scottsdale

Scottsdale and the fine arts make a well-matched couple. Start at the **Scottsdale Civic Center Mall**. (This is a "mall" in the sense of "open public space" not a shopping center.) Spend some time wandering the delightful maze of lush gardens, ponds, fountains and sculptures. Be sure to stop for a photo at the **Robert Indiana "Love" Sculpture**, which you've probably seen on postage stamps.

On one side of the plaza, just beyond the **Performing Arts Center**, you'll find the edgy **Scottsdale Museum of Contemporary Art**. With a wide variety of ever-changing exhibits, the museum explores modern culture through art and architecture. Manageably small, you can easily tour the three galleries in under an hour. *Info: 7374 East Second Street. Tel. 480-994-ARTS. www. smoca.org. Open Tuesday, Wednesday, Sunday 12pm-5pm. Thursday-Saturday 12pm-9pm. Admission: $7 adults, children under 15 free. Free on Thursdays.*

## Lunch & A Show

Enjoy lunch indoors or out at **AZ88** (see *Where to Eat*) on the mall. The restaurant is right in front of the outdoor stage that features music many weekends and **Native American dance and music performances** (called Native Trails) in the winter and spring. *Info: scottsdaleperformingarts.org.*

A ten-minute drive north on Scottsdale road is the bizarre, otherworldly **Cosanti Foundation**. The founder, Paolo Soleri, defined his work as arcology – a type of architecture integrated with the ecological workings of its surroundings. You can tour earthformed concrete structures amid a natural desert setting that includes cactus, palo verde, and olive trees. Most interesting are the **cause bells**, which are cast bronze and ceramic wind chimes made in honor of various worthy causes around the world. Take one home and enjoy the unique tones as a reminder of your trip to Arizona. *Info: 6433 Doubletree Ranch Road. Tel. 480-948-6145. www.arcosanti.org. Open 11am-5pm daily. No admission fee.*

Scottsdale is known for its **world-class spas**, so what better way to enjoy your time here than getting pampered at one of the luxury resorts in town. Even if you're not staying at the resorts, you can enjoy their spa packages and many times have access to their swimming pools and other facilities. Some of the best pampering can be found at the **Fairmont Princess**, the **Hyatt Gainey**, and **The Phoenician** (see *Where to Stay*.)

The **Scottsdale Arts District**, in the heart of Old Town, is great if you love art. Focus on the galleries of **Marshall Way** if you prefer contemporary, or those on **Main Street** for western and Native American works. Every Thursday from 7pm-9pm the galleries stay open late for **Art Walk**, an open-house of sorts where you can tour the galleries, learn about the artists, and talk to gallery owners. *Info: Between Fifth Avenue and Main Street in Old Town Scottsdale. Tel. 480-990-3939. www.scottsdalegalleries.com.*

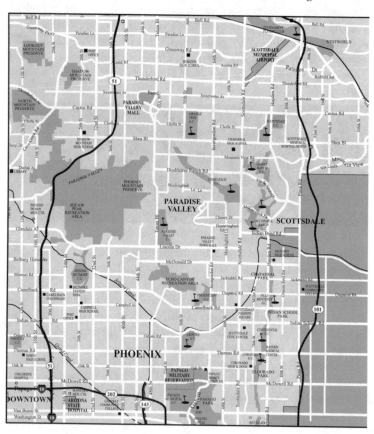

About 20 minutes northeast of downtown Scottsdale you can visit **Frank Lloyd Wright's remarkable Taliesin West**. Wright, arguably one of the most important architects in American history, established a winter "camp" in Scottsdale in 1937 for his apprentices. He and his charges literally created Taliesin West out of the desert by collecting rocks and sand for the construction of a complex of buildings that served as his personal home, studio and architectural campus until his death in 1959. There

are a variety of tour options, but first-time visitors should take the one-hour **Panoramic Tour**. Guides explain how the architecture relates to the desert and provide a general overview of Wright's basic design theories. It's amazing to see how each building and outdoor space was very purposely constructed to illustrate his ideas. *Info: Located at Cactus Road and Frank Lloyd Wright Boulevard. Tel. 480-860-2700. www.franklloydwright.org. Open daily 9am-4pm. Tour prices vary from $19 to $75 for adults.*

About ten minutes west of Taliesin is **Kierland Commons**, a bucolic open-air shopping mall with a number of wonderful eateries. Try **Zinc**, an excellent Parisian bistro complete with a real zinc bar; **NoRTH**, specializing in modern Italian dishes; **RA**, a tasty sushi spot; or the new branch of popular **Postino WineCafe**, featuring locally-sourced food and a long wine list.

### Salt River Entertainment Complex
Located on the Salt River Pima Maricopa Indian Reservation just across the street from the Scottsdale border at Loop 101 and Via de Ventura, this growing complex offers a number of entertainment opportunities. The newly opened **OdySea Aquarium** (*www.odyseaaquarium.com*) is the latest offering, featuring a host of marine exhibits. Also in the area are the **Butterfly Wonderland** (*butterflywonderland.com*), with interactive exhibits for kids, and the **Odysea Mirror Maze** (*www.odyseamirrormaze.com*) with both mirror and laser mazes.

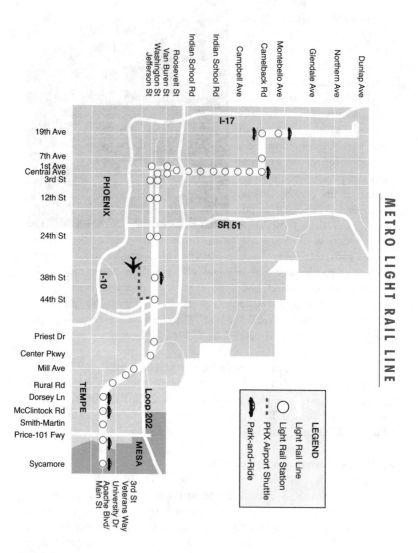

**Tempe**
The main event in Tempe is **Arizona State University**. (ASU is just south of the 202 and west of the 101 along the Rio Salado.) Start your tour at Rural and Apache (closest Light Rail Stop Rural and University) at the Visitor Information Center. Don't miss the **Gammage Auditorium**, Frank Lloyd Wright's last public structure; and the **Arizona State University Art Museum**, with its collection of American and European works. You'll also want to saunter down the school's main drag, **Mill Avenue**, to get a sense of the current college scene. If you have time, make it a priority to have a drink or meal at the nearby **House of Tricks**, the best and most pleasant restaurant in Tempe (see *Where to Eat*).

## PHOENIX AREA EXCURSIONS
**Apache Trail & Tonto National Monument**
The nearby **Apache Trail** is **one of the most beautiful drives** in this part of the state. Built in 1905 during the construction of the Roosevelt Dam, the route closely follows the path once taken by the Apache Indians as they traveled through the canyons of the Salt River. You'll experience outstanding mountain, lake, and desert scenery as well as historic towns and ruins over the course of the 190-mile drive. To get there, follow US60 east of town to AZ88 and the town of **Apache Junction**.

Continue on AZ88 into the heart of the scenic views (and the curves). Several beautiful lakes link together like a chain of pearls across the collarbones of the Superstitions. You can stop for a 90-minute tour of **Canyon Lake** on *The Dolly Steamboat*, but if you do you might not have time to view the rest of the attractions on the loop in one day. *Info: Canyon Lake Marina and Campground. Tel. 480-827-91444. www.dollysteamboat.com. Daily 12pm and 2pm. $23 adults, $12 children 5-12. Dinner and astronomy cruises available as well.*

You will reach a stretch, just past **Tortilla Flat**, where you have 26-miles of unpaved road. Just take it slowly and you'll be fine. The highlight here is **Fish Creek Canyon** with its 2,000-foot multicolored walls. The road returns to pavement at the impressive **Roosevelt Dam**. Four miles beyond the dam is the worthwhile **Tonto National Monument** (*see photo on next page*). A well-preserved, two-story cliff dwelling that dates from the 14th century, the ruins were built by the Salado Indians into a natural cave about 350 feet above the visitor's center. There is a steep, paved one-mile roundtrip trail to the lower cliff dwelling that you can visit on your own. Guided hikes to the upper dwelling must be reserved in advance, take three

hours, and involve a three-mile hike. You can also simply enjoy the view of the dwelling from below. Many of the objects recovered from the dwellings can be seen in the visitor's center museum. *Info: Four miles east of Roosevelt Dam on AZ88. Tel. 928-467-2241. www.nps.gov/tont/index.htm. Open daily 8am-5pm. Admission $5 per adult, children free.*

The final 28 miles of the Apache Trail are a much easier drive than the first part of the trip. You've got another chance to walk through a Salado Indian pueblo at the **Besh-Ba-Gowah Archaeological Park**, where some of the dwellings have been restored and furnished. You even get to climb ladders to the upper stories of the dwelling if you'd like. There is also an interesting museum that documents Salado life in the 13th century. *Info: South of Globe off of US60. Tel. 928-425-0320. www.globeaz.gov/visitors/besh-ba-gowah Open daily 9am-5pm. Admission $5 for adults, 12 and under free.*

**Globe**, a historic mining town, is a good option for a late lunch. The city was supposedly named after a globe-shaped piece of silver found nearby. Exit on Broad to downtown Globe and stop at **La Casita Café** for a memorable taste of Mother Salustia Reynosa's original recipes. The cheese crisp is classic Arizona-Mex and the enchiladas are fantastic. *Info: 470 N Broad St. Tel 928-425-8462.*

## Lost Dutchman Hike

There are some excellent hikes in the **Superstition Mountains** that loom to the east. They are best accessed through the nearby **Lost Dutchman State Park**, so you can stop for a scramble if you are so inclined. *Info: 6109 N. Apache Trail. Tel. 480-982-4485. azstateparks. com/Parks/LODU. Open daily sunrise to 10pm. Admission $7 per vehicle.*

Heading back towards Phoenix on US60 is the stunning **Devil's Canyon**, characterized by very jagged and rocky ridges and unusual pointed formations. Three miles west of Superior the **Boyce Thompson Southwest Arboretum** is tucked into the base of Picketpost Mountain. A staggering variety of desert vegetation has been gathered from all over the world and is beautifully planted on the Arboretum's 420 acres. The easy paths that meander through the property cover desert terrain as well as areas with an unexpected amount of dense vegetation home to numerous colorful birds. *Info: US60 milepost 223. Tel. 520-689-2811. arboretum.ag.arizona.edu. Open daily in summer 6am-3pm and 8am-4pm the rest of the year. Admission $10 adults, $5 children 5-12.*

Jump back on US60 and you'll return to the Valley in about 45 minutes.

### Historic Florence & Casa Grande Ruins National Monument

Head south on I-10 to exit 185 and follow the signs east to the **Casa Grande Ruins National Monument**. (Do not follow the signs to the town of Casa Grande.) Casa Grande was the first archeological site to be preserved by the federal government. Meaning the "Big House," Casa Grande was constructed around 1350 by the **Hohokam Indians**. The settlement was abandoned approximately a hundred years after it was built for reasons unknown.

Casa Grande is of historical importance because it represents the ultimate architectural achievement of Hohokam society. The monument consists of a large central structure that is four stories high and built out of layers of mud. This is surrounded by the remains of a walled village. You can take either a self-guided or ranger-conducted walk through the ruins. It will take about an hour to tour the monument and visit the on-site museum.

*Info: AZ87. Tel. 520-723-3172. www.nps.gov/cagr/index.htm. Open daily 9am-5pm. Admission $5 adults, children under 15 free.*

From Casa Grande, take AZ287 to **Florence**, an old west town that has retained much of its historic flavor. There are over 150 buildings here that are on the National Register of Historic Places. Take the time to walk down Main Street and you'll feel like you have walked back in time. (Main and 8th Ave.)

If you're interested in the history of the area, stop at the excellent **Pinal County Historical Museum** at 715 S. Main. It's small, but has many interesting items such as buckskin playing cards and beautiful furniture crafted from cholla and saguaro cactus.

For lunch, head straight across the street from the Pinal Country Museum to the **LB Inn** at 695 S Main for some simple but **delicious Mexican food**. (They also serve burgers and sandwiches.) Request a table by the fountain on the large back patio and order up the daily special.

## WHERE TO STAY
### Arizona Biltmore Resort & Spa $$$
No other hotel in the Valley has as much historical significance as the Frank Lloyd Wright-influenced and partially-designed Biltmore. This playground of presidents and movie stars features unique geometric blocks and organic nature-influenced design. Spectacular grounds, with beautiful gardens ablaze with color, mountain vistas, and wicker lounge chairs for relaxing. Tours are highly recommended to appreciate the hotel's storied past. Enjoy the present at the eight pools, one with a long water slide and swim-up bar, two 18-hole golf courses, seven tennis courts, spa, full gym, steam room, and several first-rate restaurants. Try Wrights for innovative cuisine and impeccable ser-

vice, Frank & Albert's for more informal fare, and the Cafe for casual food with outstanding terrace views. Rooms are large and comfortable. Villas available. Ocatilla rooms include a dedicated concierge, complementary beer and wine in the lounge, and daily breakfast. Ask about the weekly speakeasy in the Mystery Room. Kids Korral program for ages 4-12. *Info: www.arizonabiltmore.com. Tel. 800-950-0086. North Central Phoenix (Camelback Corridor) near the Phoenix Mountain Preserve: 2400 E Missouri Ave. 739 Rooms/Suites.*

### Fairmont Scottsdale Princess $$$

A luxurious larger-than-life hacienda situated on over 450 acres awaits you at the Princess. Designed in lovely Mexican-colonial style, the hotel features

graceful arches and covered colonnades serving as walkways. Most spectacular is the large area from the main entrance back to the swimming pool – water cascades down pyramid-like structures while bridges lead over artificial streams. The large rooms boast separate sleeping and living areas. Casitas and suites feature fireplaces. Bourbon Steak, featuring contemporary American cuisine that includes all natural, organic beef, is the highlight of the dining options, while the indoor-outdoor Plaza Bar draws hipsters from all over Scottsdale. La Hacienda offers authentic Mexican cuisine in a delightful ambiance. Two golf courses, seven tennis courts, six swimming pools (the newest and largest one with a real white-sand beach), two water slides, a fitness trail, croquet and even fishing will keep you entertained, while the spa is a great place to relax. *Info: www.fairmont.com/scottsdale. Tel. 800-223-1818. North Scottsdale. 7575 East Princess Drive. 651 rooms.*

### Hyatt Regency Scottsdale at Gainey Ranch $$$

Low key and classy, the Hyatt is all about understated elegance. With a secluded palm tree and cactus-lined driveway, the low-rise façade just hints at the beauty inside. The multi-level atrium lobby, with retractable glass doors, opens out to the magnificent grounds. The hotel features an outstanding collection of paintings, statues, and other works of art that fit with the elegant architecture. One of the hotel's main attractions, the newly refurbished 2.5 acre water playground, consists of ten interconnected swimming pools, a sandy beach, a three-story waterslide, glass and marble water cascades, water volleyball and basketball, rental cabanas, and plenty of shaded lounging areas. The rooms, decorated in a serene modern style,

---

### Off-Season Specials

You can get some fantastic deals in the off season. Rooms that go for $350 per night in the spring drop to $150 or less in the summer. Or, ask about the special golf or spa packages that many of the resorts offer.

---

are large and comfortable. Those on the Regency floors include breakfast and snacks. If you need more than one room, inquire about the casitas, which offer a spacious living area, wrap-around patios, and a roof-top terrace complete with telescope. With a wide variety of restaurants, featuring Italian, Southwestern, and Japanese cuisine, the hotel offers something for every palate. Recreation opportunities include a gym, tennis courts, 27 holes of championship golf, and trails for jogging or biking. Camp Hyatt offers fun activities for kids. The wonderfully tranquil Spa Avenia is a destination in itself, offering relaxation areas, a secluded Celtic mineral pool for spa patrons, and a wide variety of spa treatments synchronized to the time of day and natural light. *Info: www.scottsdale.hyatt.com. Tel. 800-233-1234. Central Scottsdale. 7500 East Doubletree Ranch Road. 493 rooms/suites.*

### The Phoenician $$$

European opulence meets southwest flavor at this luxury resort known for its distinguished service. Combines truly spectacular architecture with the natural beauty of its desert and mountain surroundings. A lush green oasis covering 250 acres. Admire the dazzling lobby, an exquisite mixture of marble, glass, and metal, highlighted by rich chandeliers, countless fountains, and numerous impressive statues. The shaded grounds are dominated by seven cascading swimming pools, a waterslide, and a tropical lagoon. Even the smallest rooms are over 600 square feet and include Italian marble bathrooms and private balconies. Suites and casitas are also available. J&G Steakhouse

features sophisticated favorites, Il Terrazzo sumptuous contemporary Italian, and Relish down-home burgers and comfort food. Outstanding services and options for those with gluten allergies. Work off that dinner on the tennis courts, the

27 holes of golf, or the hiking and biking trails. The Centre for Well-Being includes a full gym as well as delightfully relaxing and rejuvenating spa services. Expanded activities, kids club, and tennis programs. *Info: www.thephoenician. com. Tel. 800-888-8234. Just a half-mile west of Old Town Scottsdale in Arcadia: 6000 East Camelback Road. 640 Rooms/Suites.*

### Royal Palms Resort & Spa  $$

Spanish-Mediterranean architecture in a truly remarkable setting. The small, tranquil, and private Royal Palms is as genteel as they come in the Valley. Tucked into the side of Camelback Mountain, the hotel still feels like the mansion it originally was. Built around quiet courtyards, the Royal Palms invites you to relax in style. The impeccably decorated guestrooms include custom furnishing, fireplaces, and private patios. T. Cook's, proclaimed the #1 restaurant in Phoenix by Food & Wine Magazine, lives up to its lofty reputation. A lovely, peaceful pool and full-service spa help visitors unwind. *Info: www.royalpalmshotel.com. Tel. 800-672-6011. Right between Old Town Scottsdale and the Camelback Corridor in Arcadia: 5200 East Camelback Road. 117 Rooms/Casitas.*

### W Hotel Scottsdale  $$-$$$

The cornerstone of Old Town Scottsdale's hip hotel market, the W exudes a cool vibe. The modern rooms, with flat-screen HDTVs, Ipod docking stations, and munchie boxes, are sleek escapes. The real attraction at the W though is the party-scene. Whether you're lounging in the Living Room (aka Lobby Bar), enjoying delicious Japanese cuisine at Sushi Roku, or seeing and being seen at the outdoor bars by the pool, you'll be part of the party. SHADE, the second-floor open-air bar, is the hottest ticket in the Scottsdale scene, day or night. The pool, with port-holes opening down to the lobby porte cochere, includes a sandy beach. There is also a fitness center and spa. *Info: www.Whotels.com/Scottsdale. Tel. 877-782-0104. Old Town Scottsdale. 7727 E Camelback Rd. 200 Rooms.*

### The Clarendon Hotel & Spa  $$

The Clarendon is a hip mid-town Phoenix boutique option located just a few blocks off the light rail line. This makes it very accessible to downtown Phoenix. Home to Tranquilo, a tasty and hip Mexican restaurant with a lively happy hour, the Clarendon is a welcoming place to stay if you like to socialize with other guests. The vibrant pool area, roof top deck, and restaurant are all wonderful places to hang out. *Info: www.theclarendon.net. Tel. 602-252-7363. Midtown Phoenix: 401 W Clarendon Ave. 105 Rooms.*

### Hotel Valley Ho  $$
Enjoying a second heyday, the remodeled Valley Ho is once again the chic place to see and be seen. Retro and cool, the décor of the hotel stems from ts original 60s look but updates it fantastically. Formerly a hangout for Hollywood's elite, the "Ho" is once again a Valley hotspot. In easy walking distance to galleries, restaurant, and bars, you can park your car and leave it. Don't miss Café Zuzu, a modern version of the 50s diner, or the OH poolside bar and cabanas. Flat screen TVs and balconies are standard in all the rooms. *Info: www.hotelvalleyho.com. Tel, 866-882-4484. Old Town Scottsdale: 6850 E. Main Street. 200 Rooms.*

### Pointe Hilton Squaw Peak Resort  $$
Kids go nuts about this hotel. With six swimming pools, multiple waterfalls, and a nine-acre water recreation area called the Hole-in-the-Wall River Ranch, there is tons for them to be excited about. Especially big hits are the waterslides, miniature golf, and the "lazy river." The tough part will be getting them back to your spacious room. Rooms are arranged in small groups around a pool or courtyard, so it doesn't seem as if you're staying at such a large hotel. Offers Coyote Camp for kids and the Toscasierra Spa for grownups. Other recreation includes golf and tennis. *Info: www. pointehilton.com. Tel. 800-947-9784. North Central Phoenix: 7677 N. 16th Street. 693 Rooms/Suites.*

### The Saguaro Scottsdale $$

This vibrant hotel, with its location on the Scottsdale civic center mall in Old Town right by the arts district, is a fun and funky player in the Scottsdale hotel scene. The striking use of bold color, designed to mimic the flowers of the dessert, gives the property

a fun and welcoming vibe. Sleek rooms include mid-century touches like old *Arizona Highways* magazines and antique cameras along with modern amenities. Two heated pools, one tranquil and the other a party spot, are surrounded by colorful cabanas perfect for lounging. The Saguaro Restaurant offers a modern take on burgers and sandwiches. This pet-friendly property also has a fitness center and spa. *Info: Tel. 877-808-2440. www.thesaguaro. com. Old Town Scottsdale: 4000 N Drinkwater Blvd. 194 rooms.*

### Best Western Plus Sundial $
This modern property features a cool, Frank Lloyd Wright-inspired design, a great location within walking distance of Scottsdale Fashion Square and Old Town, and a reasonable price. Located across the street from the W, it's a good spot for nightlife as well. Amenities include wi-fi, outdoor heated pool, hot tub, and complementary breakfast. *Info: Tel. 800-780-7234. www.bestwestern.com. Old Town Scottsdale: 7320 E Camelback Rd. 54 rooms.*

### Comfort Suites Scottsdale $
When you're looking for inexpensive lodging in Scottsdale you have to realize that everything is relative. You're not going to get fancy sheets or 5-star service, but what you get here is a good location right by Old Town Scottsdale and a decently large room for the price. Breakfast included. Indoor pool. Outdoor hot tub. Free wi-fi. *Info: www.choicehotels.com. Tel. 877-311-5661. Old Town Scottsdale. 3275 N. Drinkwater Blvd. 60 rooms.*

### Motel 6 Scottsdale $
Yes, it's a Motel 6, but the location is outstanding and the price couldn't be better for Scottsdale. An easy walk to shopping galore at Scottsdale Fashion Square and Old Town. Small pool with mountain views. *Info: www. motel6.com. Tel. 800-466-8356. Old Town Scottsdale: 6848 E Camelback Road. 122 Rooms.*

## WHERE TO EAT
### Cowboy Ciao $$$
They call it "Modern American" food, but it's really an inventive union of Italian and Old West cuisine that simply clicks. The restaurant, decorated n Border Baroque style, is welcoming and fun. Dinner will be as entertaining as it is delicious, especially if you sample some of the generous pours from the extensive (over 2,200 offerings) wine list. Yet the food remains the center of attention. Don't miss the mushroom pan fry or the corn nut scallops. The Bacon Doughnuts justify your entire trip to Phoenix. *Info: Tel.*

*480-946-3111. www.cowboyciao.com. Old Town Scottsdale: 7133 E. Stetson Dr. Open daily lunch and dinner.*

### House of Tricks $$$

Located in side-by-side historic homes with a sprawling grapevine-canopied patio, House of Tricks is a wonderful surprise tucked into student-laden Tempe. (Hey, professors and visiting parents have to eat somewhere.) It's so pleasant you can't go wrong here for lunch, dinner or even just happy hour. The menu takes advantage of seasonally fresh ingredients and includes seafood, poultry, and fine meats, as well as vegetarian selections. *Info: Tel. 480-968-1114. www.houseoftricks.com. Tempe (near ASU): 114 East 7th Street. Closed Sunday. Reservations recommended.*

### Lon's at the Hermosa $$$

You come to Lon's first for the incredible setting and ambiance and return again and again for the food. Housed in a historic hacienda (now the Hermosa Inn) in Paradise Valley, the wood and adobe dining room transports you to an earlier century. Even better however, is eating outside on the expansive patio, where you're surrounded by incomparable desert and mountain scenery. The menu, featuring inventive American cuisine and freshly harvested local produce, will make everybody happy. *Info: Tel. 602-755-7878. www.hermosainn.com/lons. Paradise Valley (between Old Town Scottsdale and the Camelback Corridor.) 5532 N. Palo Cristi Road. Open nightly for dinner and on weekdays for lunch. Reservations recommended.*

### T. Cook's $$$

Located in the unrivaled mansion setting of the Royal Palms Hotel, T. Cook's offers superb Mediterranean cuisine influenced by northern Spain and central Italy. Voted the best restaurant in the Valley by *Food & Wine Magazine*, T. Cook's is a favorite for special occasions and celebrations (including a few anniversary dinners of yours truly). *Info: Tel. 866-579-3636. www.royalpalmshotel.com/restaurant. Between the Camelback Corridor and Old Town Scottsdale in Arcadia: 5200 East Camelback Road. Open daily for breakfast lunch and dinner. Reservations recommended.*

## Vincent's on Camelback $$$

Exquisite cuisine and service in a memorably romantic atmosphere. There's a hint of both French and southwest in everything on the menu – a most appealing and flavorful combination despite how it might sound. Many entrees are mesquite grilled. Especially delicious are the grilled rack of lamb with thyme, rosemary, garlic and spicy pepper jelly and the corn ravioli with white truffle oil. If a fancy French  meal is too heavy on your wallet, try the attached Vincent's Market Bistro. You can sample much of the same cuisine at a fraction of the cost. *Info: Tel. 602-224-0225. www.vincentsoncamelback.com . Camelback Corridor: 3930 East Camelback Road. Closed Sundays. Reservations recommended.*

## Barrio Café $$

For delicious southern Mexico cuisine in a very lively atmosphere, don't miss the justifiably popular Barrio Café. The guacamole prepared tableside is outstanding, as is the cochinita pibil, Yucactan-style pork roasted with achiote and oranges. You'll probably have to wait a while for a table, but half the fun is ordering drinks and appetizers in the tiny bar. This restaurant is so popular they have opened two more branches. If you are staying in Scottsdale, check out the Café's sister restaurant the Barrio Queen at the Scottsdale Waterfront or try the newly opened Barrio Café Gran Reserva (where you can make reservations) at 1301 W. Grand Ave in Phoenix. *Info: Tel. 602-636-0240. Central Phoenix: 2814 N. 16th Street (1 1/2 blocks south of Thomas.) www.barriocafe.com. Open for dinner Tuesday-Sunday and lunch Tuesday-Friday. Sunday Brunch. Closed Mondays. No reservations.*

## Chelsea's Kitchen $$

Once an old roadhouse, this landmark building on the canal in Arcadia is now one of Phoenix's most enjoyable eateries. With a fantastic patio and nice open floor plan, the restaurant is comfortable yet chic at the same time. While it's a hot spot for couples, it's also great for families because it's plenty lively. Try the lobster tacos or the melt-in-your-mouth braised short ribs. *Info: Tel. 602-957-2555. www.chelseasaz.com. Arcadia (between Old Town Scottsdale and the Camelback Corridor): 5040 N. 40th Street ( just north of Camelback.) Open daily for dinner only. No reservations.*

### La Grande Orange Pizzeria and Grocery $$

It's a pizzeria, a grocery store, a cafe, a coffeehouse, and a wine store – if you can't make everybody in your group happy here then you can't make them happy anywhere. A popular neighborhood haunt, La Grande Orange features casual seating outdoors and a contemporary urban vibe inside. With great pizza, pastries, sandwiches, salads, and breakfasts you can't go wrong any time of day. (The pizzeria is only open at dinner however.) *Info: Tel. 602-840-7777. www.lagrandeorangegrocery.com. Arcadia (between Old Town Scottsdale and the Camelback Corridor): 40th Street & Campbell at 3939 East Campbell. Open daily. No reservations.*

### Pizzeria Bianco $$

Calling Pizzeria Bianco a "pizza joint" is a bit like calling a Stradivarius "a nice fiddle." Owner Chris Bianco was named by the James Beard Foundation as the best chef in the southwest – for his pizza! Made with homemade crust, fresh mozzarella, and herbs straight from the garden, these are pizzas you will dream about when you're back home. There is always a wait, but luckily there are picnic tables outside where you can bring wine from Bar Bianco next door and enjoy the historic atmosphere of Heritage Square. *Info: Tel. 602-258-8300. www.pizzeriabianco.com .Downtown in Heritage Square: 623 E Adams. Open for dinner only. Closed Sundays. Reservations for groups of 6-10 only.*

---

### Best Gourmet Pizza

Besides La Grande Orange and Pizzeria Bianco, two other great gourmet pizza restaurants are **Cibo** (*603 North Fifth Ave at Fillmore St, Tel. 602-441-2697*) and **Grazie** (*6952 E Main St, Scottsdale, Tel. 480-663-9797*).

---

### Scottsdale Waterfront and SouthBridge Restaurants on the Canal $-$$$

The section of the Arizona Canal just west of Scottsdale Road and South of Camelback Road is known as the Waterfront. A number of fine restaurants can be found along the banks on both sides of this canal. On the north side, adjacent to Scottsdale Fashion Square, you'll find:

- **Wildfish Seafood Grille $$** – Upscale seafood. Tel. 480-994-4040.
- **Olive & Ivy $-$$** - Tapas-like Mediterranean dishes and pleasant outdoor seating. Tel. 480-751-2200.

- **Culinary Dropout $-$$** - Fun gastro-pub that's nice for happy hour. Tel. 480-970-1700.
- **Sauce $** - Great for quick pizza or salad. Tel. 480-321-8844.

On the south side of the canal, along E. Stetson, you'll find the Southbridge area, which includes:

- **Herb Box $-$$** - Featuring farm-stand fresh ingredients, the Herb Box is a treat for breakfast, lunch or dinner. Tel. 480-289-6160.
- **Barrio Queen $$-$$$** - Authentic interior Mexican food and an extensive tequila list. Fantastic and tasty tacos. Breakfast served until 3pm. Tel. 480-656-4179.

### AZ88 $

With a fantastic location right on the Scottsdale Civic Center Mall, the patio of AZ88 overlooks fountains, gardens, and quite often, shows at the amphitheater. With a simple but tasty menu of salad, sandwiches, and burgers, the restaurant draws a crowd that changes as the night progresses. The families give way to couples and groups of singles, which give way to partiers with the munchies the later it gets. *Info: Tel. 480-994-5576. www. az88.com. Old Town Scottsdale: 7353 Scottsdale Mall. Open weekdays for lunch and dinner. Open for dinner only on weekends. No reservations.*

### The Café at the Biltmore $

With open air seating under the portico, The Café at the Biltmore is a great way to experience a luxury resort without harming your wallet. It's all about the ambiance. You look out over the incredible manicured gardens to see the peaks of the Phoenix Mountain Preserve beyond. You can wait for a server, but it's easier to go inside the café and order a sandwich or salad yourself. They'll bring it out to you when it's ready and in the meantime you will have been mesmerized by the view. *Info: Tel. 602-381-7632. www. arizonabiltmore.com. North Central Phoenix (Camelback Corridor) near the Phoenix Mountain Preserve: 2400 E Missouri Ave. Open daily for breakfast and lunch. No reservations.*

### Palette $

Featuring a seasonally-focused menu, Palette, inside the Phoenix Art Museum, is a welcoming place to relax and eat lunch. Gourmet sandwiches and salads, as well as hand-crafted cheeses and Arizona boutique beers, make it worth a stop even if you're not going to tour the museum. *Info:*

*Tel. 602-257-2191. Downtown at Central and McDowell: 1625 N Central Ave. Open Tuesday-Sunday. No reservations.*

### Postino Winecafe $

Postino is like a commercial for how happy hour is supposed to be – pretty people drinking excellent wines and noshing on tasty fare. Housed in what used to be the Arcadia post office, the building has a glass paneled garage door that is rolled up in nice weather to create a wonderful indoor/outdoor effect. Postino serves excellent light dishes of bruschetta, salads, and panini and of course, the wine is divine. Even though it is hip, it is not really a place to see and be seen. It's more a place to come and enjoy. (And now those staying in North Scottsdale can enjoy another branch of Postino opened at the Kierland Commons.) *Info: Tel. 602-852-3939. www.postinowinecafe. com. Arcadia (between Old Town Scottsdale and the Camelback Corridor): 40th Street & Campbell at 3939 East Campbell. Open daily. No reservations. There is also branches on Central Avenue near Camelback and in Gilbert.*

### Citizen Public House $$

This gastro-pub has been a winner with diners and critics alike since it opened. With an extensive and inventive cocktails list, a prime location in Old Town Scottsdale, and a menu featuring original takes on traditional pub favorites, this restaurant will not steer you wrong. The pork belly pastrami and the chopped salad (which has its own Facebook page) are two musts. *Info: Tel. 480-398-4208. www.citizenpublichouse.com. Scottsdale Old Town. 7115 E. 5th Ave. Open Daily. Reservations available.*

### The Fry Bread House $

No trip to Arizona would be complete without sampling some authentic Indian Fry Bread. This deep-fried dough can be served either savory (think Fry Bread Tacos with green chili salsa) or sweet (with honey and powdered sugar.) *Info: Tel. 602-351-2345. Central Phoenix near Indian School Rd. and 7th Street. 1003 E Indian School Road. Open Monday-Saturday*

## SHOPPING

There are malls all over Phoenix, but a few deserve special mention. They offer not only shopping, but also excellent dining and even nightlife choices. The most impressive is **Scottsdale Fashion Square** (*www.fasionsquare.com*) near Old Town Scottsdale at Camelback and Scottsdale Road. With over 225 retailers, including Barneys New York and Neiman Marcus, it's the largest mall in the southwest.

If you are in the Camelback Corridor and are in need of a little retail therapy, try **Biltmore Fashion Park** at Camelback and 24$^{th}$ St. (www.shopbiltmore. com) With an open-air park setting, the set up allows people to enjoy the weather while shopping.

If you're in North Scottsdale you can enjoy **Kierland Commons**, a "main street" shopping experience at Scottsdale Road and Greenway (www. kierlandcommons.com). Set up to mimic the tranquility of walking from store to store in a little town, Kierland is centered around a central square and fountain.

For **specialty shops and unique boutiques**, Scottsdale is tops. The Borgata, at Scottsdale Road and Lincoln, offers many one-of-a-kind stores, as does **Old Town Scottsdale** itself, especially on 5$^{th}$ Ave. Don't overlook the **museum gift stores** at the Heard, Phoenix Art Museum and Scottsdale Museum of Contemporary Art for some great finds.

Popular **resale stores** include **My Sisters Closet** (*www.mysisterscloset.com*), with locations in Scottsdale and the Camelback Corridor, for **high-end items**. Look to **Buffalo Exchange** in Tempe for more campus-oriented styles (*www.buffaloexchange.com*).

Old Town Scottsdale is also the place to shop for **Native American** as well as **Western** items. The area just east of Scottsdale Road and south of Indian School has many stores that fit this bill. Try **Atkinson's Trading Post** on Brown, and **Gilbert Ortega Galleries** on East 5$^{th}$ Ave.

## NIGHTLIFE & ENTERTAINMENT
While the hot spots constantly change, their general locations tend to stay more or less the same. The hopping Scottsdale nightlife can generally be found in Old Town. Perennial favorites include **Maya Day and Nightclub** (*mayaclubaz. com*) and **The Mint** (*www.themintaz.com.*).

The hotel lobby bars at the "hip" hotels are also well worth a visit. **Shade**, the poolside bar at the W Hotel, is happening night and day. You can also try the **Zuzu Lounge** at the Valley Ho, or the **Jade Bar** at the Sanctuary Resort. The lobby bar at the **Hyatt Gainey** is fantastic for casual drinks outside or in. The **Kazbar**, a speakeasy with an unmarked door on Stetson, is a must for late-night drinks and live music. (*www.kazbar.net.*) If you want to experience a full-on country bar, don't miss the **Rusty Spur Saloon** (*www.rustyspursaloon.com*) on Main St.

One of the hottest games in town is **Top Golf** (*topgolf.com/us/riverwalk*), a driving range/bar on the reservation just east of Scottsdale. Private hitting bays with chip-embedded golf balls as well as a large outdoor lounge.

**Downtown Phoenix** is home to plenty of bars capitalizing on their proximity to major professional sports teams. Try **Dan Majerle's Sports Grill** (*www. majerles.com*) for hoops and happy hour or **Alice Cooper'stown** (*www. alicecooperstown.com*) where jocks and rock meet. The ambiance at the **Bar Bianco** on Heritage Square is a sure hit as well (*www.pizzeriabianco.com*).

If **gambling** is your pleasure, you won't have to drive far in the Valley to find a casino. The largest option is **Casino Arizona**, with two Valley locations. The older one is located at 101 and McKellips just south of Scottsdale, while the newer one can be found at 101 and Indian Bend just east of Central Scottsdale. Part of the Talking Stick Resort, the Indian Bend location is more convenient to many Scottsdale hotels (*www.casinoaz.com*). Other casinos can be found in Fountain Hills, in Gilbert, and also Apache Junction.

If you'd like to find time for a little culture at night, there are a number of excellent locations for the **performing arts**. Check websites before you visit for up-to-date information. The biggies include the **Gammage Auditorium** at ASU in Tempe (*www.asugammage.com*), the **Herberger Theater Center** in Phoenix (*www.herbergertheater.org*), the **Scottsdale Center for the Performing Arts** (*www.scottsdaleperformingarts.org*), and the outstanding **Mesa Arts Center** (*www.mesaartscenter.com*). The **Arizona Opera** (*azopera. org*) has a sparkling new opera center in downtown Phoenix.

## SPORTS & RECREATION
### SPECTATOR SPORTS
#### Baseball
There's always something happening sports-wise in the Valley. Perhaps the biggest draw is the **Cactus League**, Major League spring training games that blanket the Phoenix metropolitan area in March (*www.cactusleague. com*). The newest stadium at **Salt River Fields**, shared by the Arizona Diamondbacks and Colorado Rockies, is a fantastic place to watch baseball in the spring sunshine.

Once the baseball season begins in earnest, you can enjoy the **Arizona Diamondbacks** at **Chase Field** in downtown Phoenix. The great thing is they close the roof and pump in AC when the temperatures rise (*arizona. diamondbacks.mlb.com*). At the college level, the ASU baseball team is a perennial powerhouse.

Other profession teams in the Valley include the **Phoenix Suns**, who play basketball in downtown Phoenix at the **US Airways Center** (*www.nba. com/suns*); the **Arizona Cardinals**, with their high tech football stadium in Glendale (*www.azcardinals.com*); the **Phoenix Coyotes** of the National Hockey League who play in Glendale also (*www.phoenixcoyotes.com*), and the **Arizona Rattlers Arena Football team** (*www.azrattlers.com*). On the women's side, the **Phoenix Mercury basketball team** plays in the US Airways Center (*www.wnba.com/mercury*).

## PARTICIPANT SPORTS
### Golf & Tennis
Phoenix is one of the golfing capitals of the United States. With over 170 courses in the Valley, it's simply **golfing heaven**. While golf here is generally expensive, keep in mind that hotels often offer golfing packages that get your price per round down to a more reasonable figure.

Some of the best public courses in the Valley include **The Boulders Resort Golf Club** north of Scottsdale in Carefree (*www.theboulders.com*); **The Phoenician Resort** between Scottsdale and the Camelback Corridor (*www.thephoenician.com*); the **TPC at Scottsdale** (*www.tpc.com/scottsdale*) home of the Phoenix Open; **Troon North** in North Scottsdale (*www.troon north.net*), and **Grayhawk**, also in North Scottsdale (*www.grayhawk.com*).

**Tennis** is available at most hotels, especially the resorts, but the **Scottsdale Athletic Club & Resort** (*www.scottsdaleresortandathleticclub.com*) offers excellent courts and training as well.

### Hiking
One of my favorite hikes with visitors is the north-central **Phoenix Mountain Preserve**. Most people come here to summit 2600 foot Piestewa Peak (formerly Squaw Peak.) Avoid the crowds by heading all the way to the end of Squaw Peak Drive and hiking **Nature Trail #304** instead. You'll get the same experience of being surrounded by Sonoran Desert without bumping into all the people. You can hike for as little as a half-mile, or put

together a route that covers as many as ten miles. *Info: Squaw Peak Drive near 24ᵗʰ Street and Glendale Ave. http://phoenix.gov/PARKS/hikephx.html. No admission fee.*

The **McDowell Sonoran Preserve** is a great escape in Scottsdale (*www.scottsdaleaz.gov/preserve/trailsplan.asp*), and the **South Mountain Preserve** in South Phoenix has tons of great trails as the largest municipal park in the country at over 16,000 acres (*phoenix.gov/PARKS/hikesoth.html*). Many visitors like the bragging rights and views that come with summiting **Camelback Mountain** (*see photo below*), the highest spot in the city (*phoenix.gov/PARKS/hikecmlb.html*).

### Biking & Walking
Great car-free biking and walking can be found on both the **Indian Bend Wash Greenbelt** in Scottsdale and the canals of Scottsdale and Phoenix. The **Indian Bend Wash Greenbelt** roughly parallels Hayden Road in Scottsdale and connects parks and golf courses along a paved pathway. The **Arizona Canal Trails**, dirt paths that run along the city's canal system, are great for long runs and casual bike rides. Ask your hotel to point you to whichever is closer.

For **mountain biking**, you should check out the single track in the parks mentioned in the hiking section, as well as the outstanding competitive tracks at the **Estrella and McDowell Regional Parks** (*www.maricopa.gov/parks*).

### Horseback Riding
Wannabe wranglers can enjoy an outing through the desert on horseback at **Spur Cross Stables** in Cave Creek (*www.horsebackarizona.com*) or **Ponderosa Stables** (*www.arizona-horses.com*) at South Mountain.

# 4. TUCSON

## HIGHLIGHTS
- **Historic Downtown** – barrio, art district

- **Arizona-Sonora Desert Museum** – gorgeous flora and fauna

- **San Xavier del Bac** – classic Spanish mission

- **Saguaro National Park** – like a parade of giant cacti

- **Bisbee** – fun Old West mining town

- **Chiricahua National Monument** – unique, breathtaking rock formations

Located in a high desert valley surrounded by mountains, Tucson enjoys a **climate somewhat cooler than Phoenix**, but equally sunny. Older than Phoenix by a long shot, Tucson's Spanish-Colonial heritage is readily evident in the adobe and pueblo-style architecture that dominates the city.

Downtown is still the vibrant heart of Tucson and should not be missed. Just to the north of downtown is the **University of Arizona** with its multiple museums and well-regarded sports teams. There is great hiking in nearby **Sabino Canyon** and beautiful outdoor attractions like **Saguaro National Park** and the **Arizona-Sonora Desert Museum**. Many excellent resorts are tucked into the mountains and foothills on the city's northern fringe.

## ORIENTATION

Located in the southern part of the state, **Tucson** is about a two-hour drive south of Phoenix on 1-10. Mountains surround the city. To get to Nogales/Mexico from Tucson, take I-10 to I-19 south.

## SEEING THE SIGHTS

### Historic Downtown

Tucson proper was founded in 1775 when a Spanish presidio, or fortified post, was established on the banks of the Santa Cruz River. While few of the original structures remain, Tucson's downtown area, with adobe buildings and Spanish street names, still retains much of its Spanish colonial flavor. Experience this *sabor latino* with a walking tour of both the **Barrio Historico** (historic neighborhood) and the **El Presidio Historic District**.

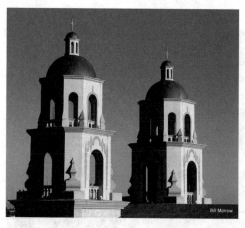
Bill Morrow

Fortify yourself before you begin with breakfast at the wonderful **Cup Café** in the historic Hotel Congress downtown. It's also a great spot for lunch and dinner featuring a menu with Asian/Latin flair (see *Where to Eat* below).

Start at the intersection of Broadway and Stone, the heart of downtown. Walk two blocks south on Stone to see the beautiful **St. Augustine Cathedral**, modeled after the Cathedral of Queretaro in Mexico (*see photo on previous page*). The original plans for the church outlined a Gothic style structure with thin pointed spires, but the spires were left unfinished for over 30 years because of lacking funds. Finally in 1928 the building was updated with a Mexican baroque look – including towers instead of spires.

Return to your starting point and head west on Broadway to the **Sosa-Carrillo-Fremont House**. This historic Mexican adobe-style dwelling has been carefully restored to look as it did in 1880 when John Fremont was the Territorial Governor. There is also an exhibit about Tucson's Hispanic pioneer families. *Info: 1151 South Granada Ave. Tel. 520-622-0956. Open Thursday-Saturday 10am-4pm. No admission fee but donations welcome.*

Continue your tour by walking over to North Main Avenue and the **El Presidio Park Historic District**. This center for the arts is where Tucson first began. There are **five historic homes** on the block as well as the Tucson Museum of Art. The homes, built between the mid-1850s to 1907, house collections of Western and Latin American art. The **Tucson Museum of Art** contains exhibits that span region's history from pre-Colombian to Western American art. It also has a great gift shop and cafe. *Info: 140 North Main Avenue. Tel. 520-624-2333. www.tucsonmuseumofart.org. Open Wednesday-Sunday 10am-5pm. (open until 8pm on Thursdays) $10 adults. Free 12 and under.*

If shopping is your thing, don't miss the **Old Town Artisans shopping area** behind the museum on Court Avenue. The historic adobe houses a number of stores around its courtyard, such as art galleries, Latin American import shops, as well as jewelers. The pleasant patio is a good place to stop for refreshments if you need a break.

And if there are kids in your group, you might want to check out the nearby **Tucson Children's Museum**. The museum promotes understanding and interest in science and history through interactive displays –the **Bodyology exhibit** is a crowd favorite. *Info: 200 S. 6th Ave. Tel. 520-792-9985. www. childrensmuseumtucson.org. Open Monday-Friday 9am-5pm. Saturday and Sunday 10pm-5pm. $8 adults, $8 children 1-18.*

**University of Arizona**
The attractive 320-acre university campus is part of what makes Tucson such

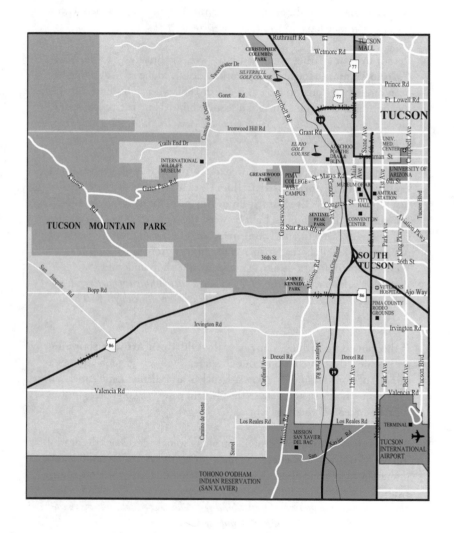

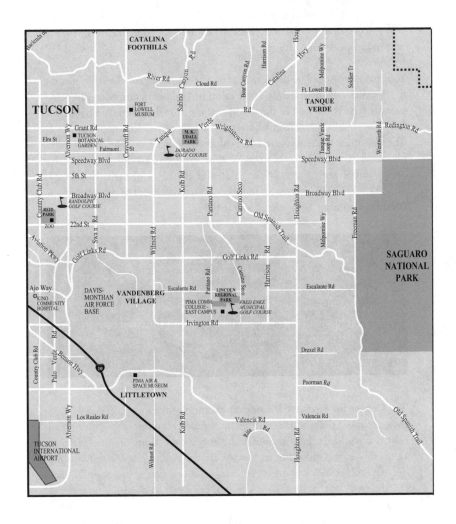

a vibrant city. In addition to walking around campus and relaxing under a shady tree, you should visit some of the attractions that include a number of museums, a planetarium, and a center for photography. The campus itself is a botanical garden of sorts featuring desert plants from all over the world. Check the local paper before you head down to the university so that you can time your visit to catch any campus sporting or cultural events that might peak your interest.

Your fist stop should be the Arizona State Museum, devoted to the cultural development of the state. The collection of Hohokam and Mogollon culture artifacts is the best in the world and some of the relics date back over 10,000 years. Scholars from all over come here to research the Southwest. The well-marked exhibits are arranged in chronological order. A huge display explains the cultures of many of Arizona's native groups, including the locally important Tohono O'odhams. Info: 1013 E. University Boulevard. Tel. 520-621-6302. www.statemuseum.arizona.edu. Open 10am-5pm Monday-Saturday. $5 adults. Free for 0-17.

## 4th Ave. Scene

Be sure to wander down 4th Avenue, right off campus, to experience the eclectic mix of shops, galleries, ethnic restaurants, and bars frequented by students. If you don't feel like walking the nine blocks of the shopping district you can take the **Sun Link Streetcar**, which connects campus to downtown Tucson via the 4th Avenue Business District.

The **Center for Creative Photography** also merits a stop. The collection includes more than 50,000 still pictures taken by photographers from all over the world. In fact, it houses the entire collections of Ansel Adams, Edward Westin, and other important artists. *Info: 1030 North Olive Rd. Tel. 520-621-7968. www.creativephotography.org. Open 9am-5pm Tuesday-Friday, 1pm-4pm, Saturday. Admission is free but a $5 donation is suggested.*

Stargazers of all ages will appreciate the newly designed **Flandreau Science Center and Planetarium**. With the goal of being a living and working laboratory designed to offer the ultimate in sensory exploration, the center has a variety of exhibits as well as a planetarium. *Info: 1601 E. University Blvd. Tel. 520-621-7827. www.flandrau.org. Hours 9am-5pm Monday* *through Thursday, 9am-10pm Friday, 10pm-10pm Saturday. 12pm-5pm Sunday. Admission $14 for adults and $7 for children 4-17.*

**West Tucson**

Tucson's wonderful **Arizona-Sonora Desert Museum** is a must on any visitor's list. Don't let the word "museum" fool you – it's really like a **zoo and botanical gardens** along with a natural history museum. Almost two miles of pathways lead through exhibits of the various ecological zones of the Sonoran Desert. You'll find more than 200 animals roaming in natural habitats, along with over 300 birds in walk-through aviaries. Some of my favorite sections are the **Woodland Mountain Habitat trail**, with its impressive mountain lion, as well as the hummingbird aviary. You'll definitely want to pause at the prairie dog village in the **Desert Grassland** section as well. Note: If you visit the museum in January-April, make reservations to eat lunch at the museums' outstanding **Ocotillo Café** (*Tel. 520-883-5705*). Using farm-fresh ingredients, the chefs prepare wonderful Arizona-Sonora regional cuisine. Open for lunch only in the winter and dinner on Saturday nights in the summer. *Info: 2021 North Kinney Road. Tel. 580-883-2702. www.desertmuseum.org. Open 8:30am-5:00pm daily (7:30am in summer). Saturdays in summer open until 10pm. $20.50 adults for visitors 13+. $8 children 3-12.*

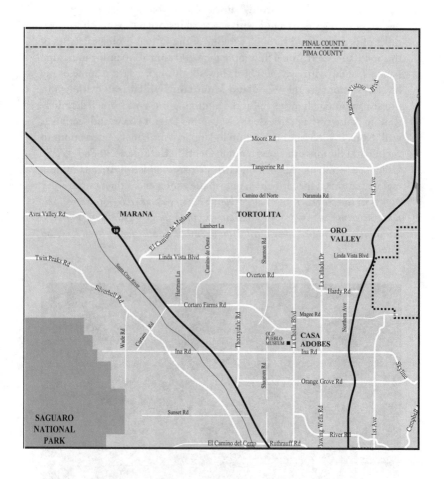

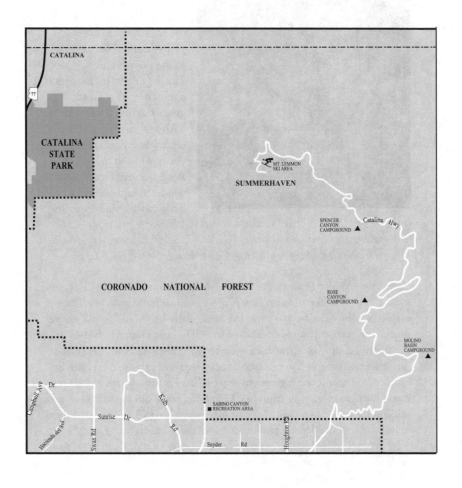

CATALINA

77

CATALINA
STATE
PARK

MT. LEMMON
SKI AREA

SUMMERHAVEN

SPENCER
CANYON
CAMPGROUND ▲          Catalina  Hwy

CORONADO    NATIONAL    FOREST

ROSE
CANYON
CAMPGROUND ▲

MOLINO
BASIN
CAMPGROUND
▲

Campbell Ave

Dr.

Kolb

SABINO CANYON
■ RECREATION AREA

Sunrise  Dr.

Hacienda del Sol

Swan Rd

Rd

Houghton Rd

Snyder    Rd

Adjacent to the museum is the western section of the outstanding **Saguaro National Park**. The **King Canyon Trail** is walking distance from the museum's parking lot. This section of the park hosts a diverse display of natural flora because of the variation in altitudes. The highlight is the park's namesake, the **Giant Saguaro Cactus**. The **Red Hills Visitor Center** explains the saguaro ecosystem in detail. If you don't want to hike, drive along Kinney Road, which winds through the park and its almost mind-boggling number of saguaros. It is literally like a forest in some places. *Info: West Tucson: Tucson Mountain District. Tel. 520-733-5153. www.nps.gov/sagu. Open 24-hours for biking or walking. Visitor Center 9am-5pm. $10 per car.*

Called the "White Dove of the Desert," **Mission San Xavier del Bac**, on the Tohono O'odham Indian Reservation southwest of town, is a Tucson highlight. The mission was founded in the late 1600s and is still active today. The current church, completed in 1797, is considered to be perhaps the finest example of Spanish mission architecture ever built. Of greatest interest are the many domes, elaborate carvings and extensive use of flying buttresses. The interior is gorgeous as well. San Xavier is worth a visit even if you have no interest in churches. Climb the small hill to the east of the mission for a nice overview of the property. San Xavier is also a good spot to indulge in some delicious, authentic Indian fry bread. *Info: Exit 92 off of I-19. Tel. 520-294-2624. www.sanxaviermission.org. Open 7:00am-5:00pm daily. No admission charge but donations are requested.*

School-age kids might like to visit the **Old Tucson Studios**, a western movie set and theme park located on Kinney Road near the Arizona-Sonora Desert Museum. A functioning movie set for westerns, it also features train rides, a carousel, and a daily gunfight. The price, to me, is a little steep for what you get, but many families and foreign tourists seem to enjoy it. *Info: Open weekends only much of the year, but daily during the winter visitor season. Check website for exact days. $18 adults, $11 children 4-11.*

### East Tucson

**Sabino Canyon**, a true oasis, is one of the highlights of the east side of town. Stop by the visitor center to see exhibits on the flora and fauna of this part of the higher Sonoran Desert before riding the tram four miles into the narrow canyon. There are stops along the way so you can get out and soak your feet in the refreshing pools of the creek. Even better, get out and hike some of the many miles of trails. *Info: Off of Tanque Verde Rd: end Sabino Canyon Road. Tel. 520-749-2861. www.sabinocanyon.com. Open 9am-4:30pm daily with tram rides every hour on the hour. $7.50 adults. $3 children 3-12.*

Very near Sabino Canyon is the interesting **DeGrazia Gallery in the Sun**. Set amid the pretty Santa Catalina Mountains, the gallery displays the paintings and sculpture of artist Ted DeGrazia. I find his paintings a little hokey, but some people love them and the setting is nice. Perhaps of greater interest is the adjacent **beautiful open-air chapel** that he built and decorated extensively with frescos. *Info: Five miles east of downtown off of Broadway: 6300 N Swan Drive. Tel. 520-299-9192. www.degrazia.org. Open 10am-4:00pm daily. Admission free.*

Another great opportunity to enjoy the Sonoran Desert can be found in the **Rincon Mountain District** of Saguaro National Park. The main draw here is the spectacular paved **Cactus Forest Drive**. This is the real heart of the Saguaro Forest, where hundreds of the tallest saguaros can easily be seen from the road. Many long trails that rise to the higher elevations of Rincon Mountain are available for hiking. *Info: East Tucson: Rincon Mountain District off of Broadway. Tel. 520-733-5153. www.nps.gov/sagu. Open 24-hours for biking or walking. Visitor Center 9am-5pm. $10 per car.*

### Gardens
If you're a fan of botanical gardens, there are two excellent options in town. **Tohono Chul Botanical Park**, a lovely 50-acre site on the north side of

town, educates the public about the historic, cultural, and environmental values of the Southwest desert regions. Stroll the tranquil trails or browse the small gallery. The park also has a lovely restaurant where you can get a great lunch. *Info: North of downtown: 7366 Paseo del Norte. Tel. 520-575-8468. www.tohono-chulpark.org. Open 8am-5pm daily. $10 adults, $3 children 5-12.*

The **Tucson Botanical Gardens** are also quite nice. Smaller and closer to downtown, the five-acre property features a collection of 16 specialty gardens. Especially nice are the Backyard Bird and Butterfly gardens. *Info: Northeast of downtown: 2150 N. Alvernon Way. Tel. 520-326-9686. www.tucsonbotanical.org. Open 8:30am-4:30pm daily. Winter $13 adults, $7.50 children 4-17. Summer $9 adults. $5 children 4-17.*

Remember **Biosphere 2**, the enclosed ecosystem designed to test the recycling capabilities of air, water, and nutrients? The experiment didn't work very well, but it was a cool concept. It's still an interesting place to visit. You too can survive inside the three-acre structure on a guided tour. The tour includes visits to the tropical savanna, the million gallon tropical ocean, and the geodesic domes that kept the whole thing from imploding.

*Info: Thirty miles north of Tucson on AZ-77. Tel. 520-838-6200. biosphere2. org. Open for tours 9:30-4pm daily. $20 adults, $13 children 6-12.*

## Take Flight!

Aviation buffs and even those just fascinated by big things will enjoy the **Pima Air and Space Museum**. The entire history of aviation in America can be traced through the museum's collection of over 200 vintage aircraft that are located along pathways and in hangers. There's even a former Air Force One. *Info: Exit 95 (Valencia Rd) off of I-19: 6000 East Valencia Road. Tel. 520-574-9658. www.pimaair. org. Open 9am-5pm daily. $15.50 adults. $9 children 7-12 (slightly cheaper in summer.)*

## DAY TRIPS SOUTH OF TUCSON

The region south of Tucson features a wonderful variety of places to see, from frontier and border towns, to caves and crazy stone formations. I've outlined four trips below. You could also combine a few of them, spending the night in one of the cities mentioned.

### Tubac & Nogales, Mexico

This adventure, which includes a visit across the border to Mexico, covers about 200 miles, almost all of which is on Interstate 19. The total drive time there and back will only take a little over three hours, giving you plenty of time to visit the sites and do some shopping on Old Mexico.

About 30 miles south of Tucson take exit 69 to Green Valley and follow the signs to the **Titan Missile Museum**. This unique facility is **a former ICBM launch site**. At one time there were more than 50 of these scattered across the US, but this is the only one that remains. It looks just like it did in its operational days, including the missile in its silo – warhead removed of course. Fascinating one-hour guided tours lead you down several flights of stairs to the control center and include a simulated launch sequence. Whatever your politics, nuclear weaponry is an important part of our nation's history. *Info: 1580 W. Duval Mine Road, Sahuarita. Tel. 520-625-7736. www.titanmissilemuseum.org. Open 8:45am-5pm Saturday. 9:45am-4pm Sunday to Friday. $9.50 adults. $6 children 7-12.*

Continue south on I-19 to Exit 34 and the small town of **Tubac**. Tubac dates prior to the arrival of the Spaniards and amazingly, was the most populous town in Arizona at one point in the middle of the $19^{th}$ century. Today it is primarily an artist's community with lots of shops. You can stop by both the **Tubac Presidio State Historic Park** (*Tel. 520-398-2252, azstateparks.com/Parks/TUPR/, $5 adults*), with a display of part of the original fort, as well as the **Tumacacori National Historic Park** (Tel. 520-398-2341, www.nps.gov/tuma, $5 16 and older), which preserves a huge Franciscan church that was started in 1800 but never finished. *Info: Both are open daily from 9am-5pm.*

## Nogales Warning

Due to post-9/11 security concerns, you now need to have a passport to get back in the US after crossing the border. At the time of the latest update of this book, the State Department is advising **against travel to Mexican border towns due to drug violence**. The State Department's website, *www.travel.state.gov*, has up-to-date alerts.

Another nice stop in Tubac is the **K. Newby Gallery & Sculpture Garden**. While the various artists displayed inside the gallery are a pleasure to visit, it's the **Monumental Sculpture Garden** that really makes it fun – especially the whimsical pair of giant rabbits. *Info: Tel. 888-389-9662. 19 Tubac Road. www.newbygallery.com. Open 10am-5pm in winter, reduced hours and closed on Tuesday in summer.*

Traveling another 20 miles south will take you to the border town of No gales, Arizona, which is located directly across from its Mexican sister city, **Nogales, Mexico**. While there isn't much to see on either side of the border, many people like to cross over to say they went to another country on their vacation (but see sidebar on previous page). Take advantage of the **busy and colorful markets** right across on the Mexican side where you can get some excellent values on high-quality artisania including clothing, pottery and jewelry. (To get to the markets, turn right on Campillo Street and walk down three blocks to Obregon.) Enjoy a meal at one of the popular restaurants on the Mexican side of the border. Try **La Roca**, *Calle Elias 91*, for wonderful food and outstanding service. Don't drive over, rather park your car in one of the guarded lots on the US side and walk across the border. It's best to be back on the US side by dark.

### Kartchner Caverns/Sonoita/Patagonia Loop
This trip takes you underground to a fascinating cave, as well as to the Arizona Wine Country and a revitalized old western town.

Take I-10 south to exit 302 and the town of Benson. From there follow the signs to AZ-90 and nine miles later you'll reach **Kartchner Caverns State Park**. The newest member of the Arizona State Parks, this large system of beautiful limestone caves was first discovered in 1974, but kept secret for 14 years. All of this time was used to prepare the caverns to minimize visitor impact on the delicate and pristine environment. Take an hour-long guided tour, whose highlights include two rooms that are more than a hundred feet high and longer than a football field, as well as the **Kubla Kahn cave** column and a **17-foot soda straw**. All of the cave walks are well lit, paved and not overly strenuous. If you only visit one cave in Arizona, this should be it, although the entry fee is quite pricey. *Info: AZ 90 south of Benson. Tel. 520-586-2283. azstateparks.com/parks/kaca/. Discovery Center Open 9am-5pm in summer and fall, 8am-6pm winter and spring. $6 per car in addition to tour fees. Tours - $23 adults. $13 children 7-13. Reservations recommended.*

Continue south on AZ-90 to the intersection with AZ-82 and head west towards the **vineyards and wineries of Sonoita**. Although Arizona and quality wine might sound like an oxymoron, there are actually some really good wines being produced in the regions. Check out **Dos Cabezas** (*doscabezaswinery.com, Tel. 520-455-5141*); *Callaghan Vineyards (www. callaghanvineyards.com, Tel. 520-455-5322*); **Sonoita Vineyards**, which also has a lovely café (*vineyardcafesonoita.com., Tel. 520-455-7449*); **Arizona Hops & Vines** (*azhopsandvines.com, Tel. 301-237-6566*); and **Rune** (*www.*

*runewines.com, Tel. 520-338-8823).* The wine is so tasty and the grasslands scenery so relaxing that you might find yourself wanting to stay a while.

Sonoita, in fact, has several good restaurants and inns. The town is an easy, romantic get-away spot for Tucsonans. Try **Café Sonoita** *(3280 AZ-82, Tel. 520-455-5278)* for a culinary treat, and **La Hacienda de Sonoita** *(34 Swanson Road, Tel. 455-5308)* for a cozy B&B if you decide to spend the night.

Head south down AZ-82 for another 12 miles to reach the little mountain town of **Patagonia**. Known both as an artists' hamlet and an international birding ground, Patagonia has attracted a unique type of citizen. Located at 4,000 feet, the town stays decently cool in the summer, so you can visit year-round. Wander the streets of town visiting the galleries and shops, or head to the two areas famous for their diversity of birdlife. Even if you're not a birder, the Nature Conservancy's **Patagonia-Sonoita Creek Preserve** *(150 Blue Heaven Road, Tel. 520-394-2400, open Wednesday–Sunday, 7:30am-4pm)* and the **Patagonia Lake State Park** *(400 Patagonia Lake Road, Tel. 520-287-6965, azstateparks.com/Parks/PALA, open 8am-10pm)* are both pleasant areas for hiking and picnics.

To get a real sense of Patagonia, all you have to do is hang out at the **Gathering Grounds Coffee Shop** for a while. This coffee, breakfast, and sandwich shop even serves dinner and has live music on weekend nights. *Info: 319 McKeown Avenue, Tel. 520-394-2097.*

### Tombstone & Bisbee

This little trip is all about the Old West. Take 1-10 to exit 303 in Benson and pick up AZ-80 for 24 miles to the historic town of Tombstone. One

of Arizona's most popular tourist destinations, it is filled with history and is especially fun for kids. You have to be willing to go with and embrace the cheesiness of it. The town appears much the same as it did in the 1880s when it was one of the most infamous of the Wild West's mining communities. Don't miss **Boot Hill**, the final resting place of a few notorious criminals, the Crystal Palace Saloon, where you can still knock back a whiskey or just enjoy a meal, or the **Bird Cage Theater** (aka brothel), which had the reputation for being one of the wildest establishments in the west. Also in town is the **OK Corral**, the location of America's most famous western gunfight between the Earp Brothers and the Clanton gang. The shoot-out is reenacted daily at 2pm.

Leave Tombstone by continuing on AZ-80 for 24 more miles to **Bisbee**. With the discovery of the Copper Queen Lode during the 1880s, Bisbee became one of the largest towns between St. Louis and San Francisco. While Tombstone is almost entirely a historic tourist site, Bisbee offers a visit to the past along with a thriving modern community. It is picturesquely located in the mountain shadows of Mule Pass and is a wonderful place to spend a few hours or even a few days.

The **Bisbee Mining and Historical Museum** on Main Street is a good place to learn about the town's past, while the **Muheim Heritage House** on Youngblood offers a look at the digs of a wealthy Bisbee businessman from 1898. Don't miss the Queen Mine at the south end of town, where former miners conduct tours in an old mining car that actually takes you into an underground copper mine. Wear a couple of layers under your mining outfit because it's 47 degrees in there (www.queenminetour.com). Most visitors spend the majority of their time walking the streets of town, stopping in at the numerous high quality shops and galleries.

Bisbee may be tiny, but there's nothing small-town about the quality of the restaurants and inns here. The delightful **Café Roka** (*35 Main St., Tel. 520-432-5153*) is the only restaurant in rural Arizona to have received a 3-Diamond rating from AAA. For a place to rest your head, try the **Canyon Rose Suites** (*27 Subway St., Tel. 866-296-7673,*) for large historical rooms, or the **Copper Queen Hotel** (*11 Howell Ave, Tel. 520-432-2216*) for a room with ghosts!

If you go to Bisbee, you should definitely pick up Richard Shelton's *Going Back to Bisbee*. It was chosen as the book for the whole state to read in 2007 and the author skillfully intertwines the history of southern Arizona with his own.

**Willcox / Chiricahua National Monument**
Take I-10 to Exit 340 and the town of Willcox, a commercial center for the many surrounding ranching operations. The town has a long history of struggles with the Apache Indians, including the famous Geronimo. Check out the **Rex Allen Arizona Cowboy Museum** (*150 N. Railroad Ave, Tel. 520-384-4583*) for all the history of Willcox's most famous native son.

The history of the Indian Wars is outlined at the **Fort Bowie National Historic Site**, about 30-miles outside of town. Established in 1862 to protect the Butterfield Stage Route from attacks by the Apache, the fort was an isolated and dangerous outpost. It's still pretty isolated today and all that's left are some crumbling walls. Signs along the trail outline other historical sites and moments. From Willcox drive southeast for 20 miles on AZ-186 to the Fort Bowie turn off, then drive eight miles on the unpaved road to the Fort Bowie Trailhead. It's another 1.5-mile walk to the ruins from there. *Info: Tel. 520-847-2500. www.nps.gov/fobo/index.htm. Open 8am-4:30pm daily. No admission charge.*

Return to AZ-186 and continue south to **Chiricahua National Monument**, one of Arizona's most beautiful but relatively unknown natural wonders. Situated in the **Chiricahua Mountains**, the area is known as the Wonderland of Rocks. The mountains rise sharply from the surrounding arid lowlands and provide a haven for many types of wildlife. Chiricahua's gray rocks often take unusual shapes and forms ranging from the sublime to the almost grotesque. Many of the park's best features can be seen from the **Scenic Drive**, an 8-mile long one-way trip to the crest of the mountain. Some of the most unusual formations include Organ Pipe Rocks, Sea Captain, and China Boy. Massai Point at the end of the road offers a fabulous panorama of tree-covered mountains and huge rock formations. There is wonderful hiking here as well, especially the Echo Canyon and Heart of Rocks trails. *Info: AZ 186. Tel. 520-824-3560. www.nps.gov/chir/. Open 8am-4:30pm daily. Open 8am-4:30pm daily. Admission free.*

Dining options are slim out here. Bring a picnic and enjoy it from one of the scenic overlooks in Chiricahua, or try **Big Tex BBQ** in Willcox. *Info: 130 E Maley St., Tel. 520-384-4423.* For lodging, don't miss the **Sunglow Ranch** (*www.sunglowranch.com*), a lovely and tranquil resort and guest ranch outside of Willcox.

## WHERE TO STAY
### Arizona Inn $$$
One of the state's oldest luxury resorts, the Arizona Inn has been pampering guests since 1930. The Inn provides a secluded and private desert oasis on 14-acres in the middle of the city. Adobe-style buildings and cottages house a small number of guests, so you get personalized service. Includes a beautifully landscaped courtyard with a rich, carpet-like lawn dotted with flowers. The warmly decorated rooms have balconies or patios and many have fireplaces. Facilities include two tennis courts, croquet, free bikes, and exercise equipment along with the heated pool. Excellent restaurants and library. *Info: www.arizonainn. com. Tel. 800-933-1093. University of Arizona Area: 2200 E. Elm St. 83 rooms.*

### Canyon Ranch $$$
More a health-retreat than hotel, the Canyon Ranch is world-famous for its spa and fitness programs. Built in harmony with the desert terrain, the accommodations range from deluxe rooms to

master suites. All are decorated in a classy southwestern style. Some visitors are here to rest, relax and rejuvenate with the many spa services, while others enjoy the extensive recreation opportunities including hiking, aquatics, tennis, and every type of yoga or fitness class you can imagine. You can even get a physical while you're here. Must be 14. Alcohol not permitted on site. Four-night minimum stay. All meals included. *Info: www.canyonranch.com/tucson. Tel. 800-742-9000. Northeast Tucson: 8600 E. Redrock Cliff Rd. 240 rooms.*

### The Lodge at Ventana Canyon $$$

The epitome of luxurious living, the spaceious suites are done in an elegant southwest motif that would be hard to improve upon. Many of the units have two bedrooms, making it a great place for families. Almost every unit overlooks the beautiful Catalina Mountains is picturesquely situated in the foothills. The many many recreational facilities include 36 holes of golf, 12 tennis courts, an expanded fitness center, and a spa. *Info: www. thelodgeatventanacanyon.com. Tel. 800.828.5701. Northeast Tucson: 6200 North Clubhouse Lane. 50 suites.*

### Tanque Verde Ranch $$$

One of the finest Arizona Guest Ranches, Tanque Verde offers something for everybody. Situated at the end of the road on 640 acres in the Rincon Mountains near Saguaro National Park, the ranch boasts a stable of over 180 horses. The main highlight of the ranch is the quality of its riding instruction. Along with the standard walking and loping trail rides, the ranch offers daily opportunities for in-depth riding instruction for both beginners and more-advanced riders. Guests can ride as many as three times a day. Non-riders

can enjoy tennis, spa-services, mountain biking, hiking, fishing, and birding. Full-suspension mountain bikes are available for rent and the single-track trails are outstanding. The heated pool and tub are great places to spend the afternoon after a long day of riding. The children's program is one of the best in the state, with riding instruction starting for kids as young as 4-years-old. The ranch was deservedly named a Top Ten Family Vacation Destination by the Travel Channel, evidenced by the number of guests who return year after year. The 74 guest units, decorated in Arizona Territorial style, range from standard rooms to suites. Most have a fireplace and patio. All meals are included in the rates. The food is quite good, especially the homemade pastries. *Info: www.tanqueverderanch.com. Tel. 800-234-3833. Northeast Tucson: 14301 E. Speedway Blvd. 74 rooms.*

**Westin La Paloma $$$**
This beautiful Spanish Mission style resort is built into the hillside at the foot of the Catalina Mountains. The grounds are gorgeous and are highlighted by the huge pool area that has a magnificent waterfall, a waterslide, and a swim-up bar and grill. Other recreational facilities include a fitness center, tennis courts, and 27 holes of golf. The guestrooms and suites are some of the best in the city, as they are huge and recently updated. Both the restaurant and lounge draw people from all over Tucson. *Info: www.westinlapalomaresort. com. Tel. 800-876-3683. North Tucson: 3800 East Sunrise Drive. 487 rooms*

**Lowe's Ventana Canyon $$$**
Spread out over almost 90 beautifully landscaped acres at the foot of the Catalinas, the property provides magnificent views of both mountain and city.
While natural flora abound, the show-case of the grounds is an 80-foot waterfall that leads into a "river" that travels serenely throughout the grounds of the resort Guest rooms are large and  attractive without being over-the-top, and some suites have full kitchens. The dining facilities are excellent as well – don't miss the Flying-V. All the recreation opportunities you could want are here – pools, health club, spa, tennis courts, and two golf courses as well as a jogging trail and nature path.

Shuttle to Sabino Canyon. *Info: www.loewshotels.com/en/Ventana-Canyon-Resort. Tel. 800-234-5117. Northeast Tucson: 7000 North Resort Dr. 398 rooms.*

### Hacienda del Sol Guest Ranch $$-$$$

The Hacienda del Sol is a cross between a luxury resort and a more casual guest ranch with great mountain views. This hotel exudes a warm Old

World charm throughout the historic hacienda-style buildings. The 31 rooms, suites, and casitas are located on a spacious 34-acres of meticulously cared for grounds. An oasis of tranquility and beauty, you could spend many hours just letting time float by as you casually wander around. Oversized rooms are the rule with the décor in keeping with the hacienda atmosphere. Swimming pool, spa, tennis and horseback riding. *Info: www.haciendadelsol.com. Tel. 800-728-6514. 5601 N. Hacienda del Sol Road. 31 rooms.*

### White Stallion Ranch $$-$$$

For a true western encounter, the White Stallion Ranch cannot be beat. The 3,000 acre ranch opened its doors to guests 1965 and has really figured out how to deliver a wonderful guest ranch experience. Located in

the Tucson Mountains adjacent to Saguaro National Park West, the White Stallion is run by some of the friendliest most down-to-earth people in the state. The riding programs are outstanding—including up to four rides daily —as are the evening entertainment sessions. The rooms, decorated in western motif, are very comfortable. The swimming pool is a favorite spot for congregating after rides. Happy hour in the bar, complete with saddles for barstools, is a fun nightly ritual, as is the evening entertainment. The meals are very good. Rates include lodging, all meals, horseback rides, and use of recreational facilities. Massages are extra. Open September-May. *Info: www.wsranch.com. Tel. 888-977-2624. Northwest Tucson: 9251 W. Twin Peaks Rd. 32 rooms.*

**El Conquistador Hilton  $$-$$$**
The El Conquistador, nestled in the foothills of the Santa Catalinas, is a wonderful resort for vacationing families who want it all. With extensive

pool and waterslide facilities, 45 holes of championship golf, tennis courts, and a spa, everyone will be more than happy. The guestrooms and suites are large and comfortable and there is a nice array of dining options. *Info: www.hiltonelconquistador.com. Tel. 800-325-7832. Northwest Tucson: 10000 North Oracle Road. 428 rooms.*

**La Posada Lodge and Casitas  $-$$**
A wonderful boutique hotel, La Posada offers quite a lot for the price. The rooms are nicely decorated in Santa Fe style, while the 12 casitas offer space and comfort. With a heated pool, exercise room, and nice Mexican restaurant on site, you get some of the amenities of a resort. *Info: www. laposadalodge.com. Tel. 800-810-2808. Northwest Tucson: 5900 North Oracle Road. 72 rooms.*

**Wayward Winds Lodge  $**
A friendly, family-run establishment, the Wayward Winds is a simple but attractive motel. All of the guestrooms overlook an attractively landscaped

courtyard, and there are even apartment units with refrigerators for a slightly higher price. Heated swimming pool, shuffleboard, and barbeque area. *Info: Tel. 800-791-9503. Northwest Tucson: 707 West Miracle Mile. 40 rooms.*

## WHERE TO EAT
### Arizona Inn Main Dining Room $$$
Featuring outstanding service and fine continental cuisine, the Arizona Inn

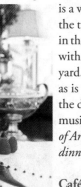

is a wonderful option if you don't want to make the trek out to some of the high-end restaurants in the foothills. The decor is Old World elegance, with cathedral ceilings, a fireplace, and a courtyard. The beef tenderloin is deliciously prepared, as is the salmon. Enjoy an after dinner drink in the dignified Audubon Bar, featuring live piano music nightly. *Info: Tel. 520-325-1541. University of Arizona Area: 2200 E. Elm St. Open nightly for dinner. Reservations recommended.*

### Café Poca Cosa $$
Definitely one of the best Mexican food restaurants in the city, Cafe Poca Cosa serves extremely imaginative, pleasingly prepared Mexican specialties. The menu changes twice daily, so you'll probably be tempted to eat here more than once. The tamales, a constant on the menu, are outstanding, as are the mole sauces. Whatever you order, you're sure to enjoy this take on Mexican high cuisine. The location on Pennington is open for lunch and dinner, while the Stone and Alameda location is open only for breakfast and lunch. *Info: Tel. 520-622-6400. Downtown. 110 E. Pennington. Closed Sunday. Dinner reservations recommended.*

### Caruso's $$
Caruso's, in the heart of 4th Ave, is somewhat of a local legend for expertly preparing Italian fare since 1938. The menu selections aren't fancy – pizza, ravioli, lasagna, manicotti – but they are tasty and served in generous amounts perfect for hungry students. Try getting a table on the beautiful patio surrounded by a refreshing row of shade trees. *Info: Tel. 520-624-5765. University of Arizona Area: 434 N. 4th Ave. Dinner served nightly except Monday.*

## City of Gastronomy

Tucson's unique regional cuisine was recognized in 2015 by UNES-CO, when the organization named the city **America's first "City of Gastronomy."** You'll find out what UNESCO was crowing about when you sample the city's food stalls, farm-to-table restaurants, and multicultural cuisine.

### Downtown Kitchen + Cocktails $$

Celebrity chef Janos Wilder created the eclectic and slightly Asian-leaning menu at this hip and urban downtown eatery. Some favorites include the outstanding fish stew and the variety of happy hour specials (called  magic hour here.) Don't miss the inventive cocktails. *Info: Downtown: 135 S. 6$^{th}$ Avenue. Tel. 520-623-7700. Opens 4pm daily for happy hour, 5pm for dinner. Reservations recommended.*

### El Charro Cafe  $$

The original El Charro on Court Avenue has been serving guests since 1922 and claims to be the oldest Mexican restaurant in the country. It's a tough call whether this or Café Poca Cosa is the best Mexican restaurant in town. You certainly can't go wrong at either one. El Charro features authentic Sonoran-style food, which is very hard to find in many part of the US. The carne seca, which they dry on the roof in the traditional manner, is outstanding. The atmosphere here is great here as well — order your margarita in a boot and you get to take the glass home for free! *Info: Downtown: 311 N Court Ave: Tel. 520-622-1922; Ventana: 6910 E. Sunrise. Tel. 520-514-1922. Oro Valley: 7725 N. Orcale. Tel. 520-229-1922.*

### Scordato Pizzeria $$-$

With a chewy-on-the-inside, crunchy-on-the-outside crust that makes you dream about the pizza here, Scordato's serves up some of the best artisan pies in the state. The roasted three mushroom pizza with Reggiono shavings is out of this world. The salads are excellent as well. *Info: Tel. 520-*

*529-2700. Catalina Foothills: 4280 N. Campbell. Ave. Open for lunch and dinner Monday-Saturday.*

### The B-line $

A wonderful bistro on 4th Ave, the B-line really can't be beat for a casual breakfast, lunch, or dinner. The homemade pies, cakes, and cookies will have you stopping by again and again whenever you're in the area, as will the catfish burro. *Info: Tel. 882-7575. University of Arizona Area: 621 N. Fourth Ave. Open 7am-9pm (10pm on Saturday).*

### Beyond Bread $

Beyond Bread does indeed go far beyond bread. Amazing salads, sandwiches and pastries make either location a great stop for any meal. The sandwiches, made on their homemade bread, are big enough for two. *Info: Eastside: 6260 E. Speedway Blvd. Tel. 520-747-7477; 3026 N. Campbell Ave. Tel. 520-322-9965. Northeast: 421 W. Ina Road, Tel. 520-461-1111. Mon-Fri 6:30am-8:00pm, Sat 7:00am-8:00pm, Sun 7:00am-6:00pm.*

### Cup Café $

Located in the historic Hotel Congress, the Cup Café is a hit for breakfast, lunch or dinner. While the menu seems to be all over the place, with Asian, Latin, and American influences, the food is top-notch. Hip Tucson hangs out here, which must explain with specialty cocktails are so outstanding. *Info: Tel. 800-798-1618. Downtown: 311 E. Congress St. Open 7am-10pm daily. (11 pm weekends.)*

### Magpies Gourmet Pizza $

When one restaurant wins a Best of Tucson award for 17 years you know they are doing something right. Magpies Pizza is that restaurant. The pizza is the draw of course, but they also serve excellent calzones and salads. Six locations around town, including the hopping 4th Ave and 5th Street loca-

---

### Hot Dogs with a Twist

Sonoran-style hot dogs, bacon-wrapped and festooned with condiments, are a unique Tucson treat. Stuffed in a bolillo bun with beans and onions, the dog is then decorated with tomatoes, mayo, and a green jalapeño sauce that represent the colors of the Mexican flag. Taste them at **El Guero Canelo**, *in south Tucson at 5201 S 12th St., east at 5802 E. 22nd St., or north at 2480 N. Oracle Rd.*

tion right by the University. *Info: Tel. 520-628-1661. University of Arizona: 605 N. 4th Ave. Sunday-Thursday 11am-9pm, Friday-Saturday 11am-10pm.*

## SHOPPING

Tucson has many opportunities to shop for southwestern and Native American items. There are also many wonderful galleries, boutiques, and even unique curio shops. If you just have to have national retailers, Tucson has malls too. **La Encantada Shopping Center** (*www.laencantadashoppingcenter. com*) features upscale shopping in the foothills of the Santa Catalinas. The **Tucson Mall** (*www.tucsonmall.com*), north of the University, is the largest and most centrally located. **Foothills Mall** (*www.shopfoothills.com*) on Ina Road in north Tucson just off of I-10 is also popular.

The **4th Avenue Shops** along Fourth Avenue between 4th and 7th Streets are great places to browse the day away. **Del Sol International Shops** (*435 N 4th Ave*) is a fantastic Indian and Southwestern store along 4th Ave. **Old Town Artisans** in the El Presidio Historic Park area may be the best place in town for Native American items.

Tucson doesn't have quite the concentration of art galleries that Scottsdale does, but among the best places are **Above & Below the Equator Gallery** at 521 4th Ave, and the already mentioned Old Town Artisans.

For one-of-a-kind furniture and outdoor items, try the shops in the **Lost Barrio warehouse shopping district**, along Park Avenue just south of Broadway Blvd.

## NIGHTLIFE & ENTERTAINMENT

The downtown **Club Congress** (*311 East Congress St., Tel. 520-622-8848, www.hotelcongress.com*) is known as THE place in town for cutting edge music and dancing. It's even been named one of the ten best rock clubs in the US. Across the street, the restored **Rialto Theater** (*318 East Congress St., Tel. 520-740-1000, www.rialtotheatre.com*) is wonderful spot to catch touring bands, comedians, and music festivals. The **Fox Theater** (*17 West Congress St., Tel. 520-624-1515, www.foxtucsontheatre.org*), another restored jewel in downtown, offers fun movies and concerts. The area around the University of Arizona has contemporary music and comedy clubs. Almost all of the resort hotels and many of the larger city hotels feature lounge entertainment.

The **Tucson Arts District galleries** stay upon until 9pm on the first Saturday of the month, which is also when many shows open. It's a nice way to see the galleries and even sometimes meet the artists. *Info: www.ctgatucson.org/first-sat.html, September through June.*

If **gambling** is your pleasure, you've got a couple of options. **Casino of the Sun** (*7406 South Camino del Oeste, Tel. 520-883-1700*) and **Desert Diamond Casino** (*7350 South Nogales Highway, Tel. 520-294-7777*) with happily help you part with your money. Both are alcohol-free by the way.

You also have nice options for the performing arts. Tucson has a **Symphony Orchestra** (*www.tucsonsymphony.org*), the **Arizona Opera** (*www.azopera.com*), **Ballet Tucson** (*www.ballettucson.org*), and the **Arizona Theater Company** (*www.arizonatheatre.org*). Check newspaper or internet for listings and Ticketmaster (*Tel. 520-321-1000*) for tickets.

## SPORTS & RECREATION
### SPECTATOR SPORTS
The biggest spectator sport action in town focuses on the **University of Arizona Wildcats**. Perennial powerhouses in basketball, golf, baseball, softball and other sports, they are strongly supported by the local populous. *Info: Tel. 520-621-5130, www.arizonawildcats.com.*

### PARTICIPANT SPORTS
**Golf**
While there are fewer courses, golfing in Tucson can hold its own with Phoenix. Some excellent courses include both the mountain and canyon courses at the **Lodge at Ventana Canyon** (*Tel. 520-577-4061*), the **Randolph Municipal North Course** (*Tel. 520-791-4336*), the **Arizona National Golf Club** (*Tel. 520-791-4336*) and the **Silverbell Municipal Golf Course** (*Tel. 520-791-4336*).

**Tennis**
Most of the major hotels and Tucson have courts and many allow non-guests to play for a higher fee. The following public tennis centers are also available: **Himmel Park** (*Tel. 520-791-3276*) and the **Reffkin Tennis Center** (*Tel. 520-791-4896*).

**Hiking**
There are many wonderful hiking opportunities in the Tucson area. See **Sabino Canyon** and both the East and West Sections of **Saguaro National**

**Park** above in *Seeing the Sights*. Another great option when it's hot outside is **Mt. Lemmon**. With an altitude of over 9,000 feet, it's a place to escape the heat during the summer months. Take the ski lift up and then hike one of the many trails that lead off from the top of the lift. *Info: Tel. 520-576-1321. www.skithelemmon.com.*

### Horseback Riding
The wonderful dude ranches around Tucson limit riding privileges to their overnight guests. A couple of stables along Oracle Road use trails in the Santa Catalina Mountains, providing a rural experience close to the city: **Pusch Ridge Stables** (*Tel. 520-825-1664, www.puschridgestables.com*) and **Walking Wind Stables** (*Tel. 520-742-4422*).

### Biking
Tucson is regularly named by *Bicycling Magazine* as one of the top cities in the country for riding. There are plenty of bike lanes and well as a couple of paved paths. Order maps at *www.tucsonaz.gov/bicycle/bikeways-footpaths-and-maps*. The roads through both sections of **Saguaro National Park** are great rides through the giants of the desert, but avoid them during peak traffic times.

# 5. North-Central Arizona

## HIGHLIGHTS

• **Flagstaff** – Museum of Northern Arizona, Snowbowl, Wupatki National Monument

• **Sedona** – Oak Creek Canyon, Chapel of the Holy Cross, adventures on red rocks

• **Prescott** – Courthouse Plaza, Whiskey Row, Granite Dells

• Wine tasting and shopping in **Cottonwood** and **Jerome**

• **Montezuma National Monument**

A **recreation wonderland**, this region is located almost entirely within National Forests. **Flagstaff**, located at the northern end of the region, is both a **gateway to the Grand Canyon** and a wonderful high-alpine getaway. It features a lively downtown, miles of hiking and mountain biking, interesting national monuments, and the most easily accessed snow skiing in the state. **Sedona**, about 30 miles south of Flagstaff, is tucked into some of the prettiest scenery in the country. Soaring red rocks, dotted with green juniper, rise and twist into unforgettable formations. You can explore these surreal formations on foot, by jeep, or on horseback and then return to a town laced with art galleries, restaurants, and fine hotels. The back-road route from Sedona winds through the pines up to the historic and picturesque mining town of Jerome, now primarily an artist colony, and then to Prescott, a town whose cowboy heritage is still very much alive.

## ORIENTATION
**Flagstaff** is located at the junction of I-17 and I-40, about 2 1/2 hours north of Phoenix. **Sedona** is south of Flagstaff off of 1-17 on AZ-89A. To get to Montezuma from Flagstaff, take I-17 to exit 289 (about 45 minutes away).

## FLAGSTAFF
Visitors love North-Central Arizona because it is so different from the Phoenix desert, yet is only a couple of hours away from the Valley. If you are limited on time, you'll want to prioritize both the **stunning red-rock vistas of Sedona** and the **pine-covered mountains in Flagstaff**.

### SEEING THE SIGHTS
With an elevation of almost 7,000 feet, Flagstaff enjoys four distinct seasons. In the winter visitors come to **ski and snowboard** in the San Francisco Mountains at **Arizona Snowbowl**. In the summer Flagstaff offers a much-needed escape from the intense Phoenix heat. Gorgeous colored leaves and stunning wildflower displays bring people to town in the fall and spring. Flagstaff is also the gateway to the Grand Canyon.

For a wonderful introduction to the entire Colorado Plateau region, head straight to the outstanding **Museum of Northern Arizona**. With exhibits that focus on the anthropology, biology, geology, and fine arts of the region, the museum offers something for everyone. They also offer various festivals throughout the year celebrating the **Navajo, Hopi, and Hispanic cultures** of the area. Kids will enjoy the short hike through the woods to a canyon with fun rocks to climb around and explore.

*Info: Three miles north of town on Highway 180 (3101 North Fort Valley Road.) Tel. 928-774-5213. www.musnaz.org. Open Monday to Saturday 9am-5pm, Sunday 12pm-5pm. Admission $12 adults; $8 children 10-17.*

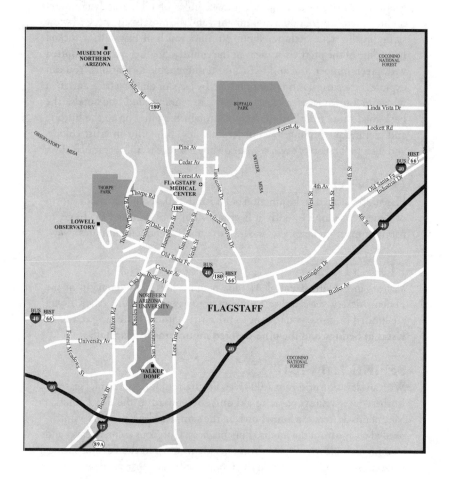

Just a few miles up Highway 180 is **Arizona Snowbowl**, a year-round getaway spot for outdoor enthusiasts, but worth a visit even if all you do it take in the views. During the summer the resort's chairlift is used to carry visitors up the mountain to panoramic vistas at 11,500 feet. (It's delightfully cool up there — take a jacket even in the summer.) There are also excellent hikes that start near the base of the chair lift as well as a disc golf course. During the winter you can enjoy skiing and snowboarding from the same spot. Great hikes near Snowbowl include:

- **Humphrey's Peak Trail** – Summit the highest point in Arizona at 12,633 feet. Difficult.
- **Kachina Trail** – One of the few trails that traverses the mountain instead of going straight up it. Moderate.
- **Veit Springs Loop Trail** – A scenic walk through the aspens that includes a visit to an old homestead and views of pictographs. Easy.

*Info: Take Highway 180 seven miles north of Flagstaff to Snowbowl Road and continue up the mountain seven miles. Tel. 928-779-1951. www.arizonasnowbowl.com. Costs and hours vary depending on activity.*

Back in town, near the Northern Arizona University campus you can visit the beautiful **Riordan Mansion State Historic Park**. This 40-room mansion was built in 1904 by a family who made their fortune in lumbering. It's a wonderful example of Arts and Crafts style architecture that features log-slab siding, volcanic stone arches, and hand-split wooden shingles. Guided one-hour tours, good to reserve in advance, take you through the many rooms with original furnishings and artifacts. Kids might find it a bit slow, but most adults really enjoy it. *Info: Half a mile north of the intersection of I-17 and I-40 at 1300 Riordan Ranch St. Tel. 928-779-4395. azstateparks.com/Parks/RIMA. Open daily in the summer 9:30am-5pm. Rest of year 10:30am-5:30pm Thursday-Monday. $10 adults and children over 14. $5.00 children 7-13. $10 adults and children over 14. $5 children 7-13.*

If you head up Milton Road from the Riordan Mansion, you'll see Mars Hill Road on the left. Take this road up to the popular **Lowell Observatory**, the place where the once-planet, now-demoted plutoid Pluto was discovered. You can tour during the day, when the astronomy exhibits and tours of the facilities are the main draws, or at night, when you can peer through telescopes at the night sky. Depending on the time of year, you may see the moon, planets, or globular and open star clusters through their 24-inch Clark Telescope. *Info: 1400 West Mars Hill Road. Tel. 928-774-3358. www.lowell.edu. Open for both day and evening tours. Extended summer hours. Admission $12 adults. $5 children 5-17.*

One of my favorite things to do in Flagstaff is simply hangout downtown on **Heritage Square**. It's a great place to get a feel for the decidedly collegiate and mountain-town vibe of the city. Everything about the square has significance, from the path detailing the history, biology, geology and anthropology of Flagstaff on a series of plaques to the redbrick railroad track design signifying the importance of the railroad. Even the benches in the Square are designed to represent Flagstaff history - the railroad, Lowell Observatory, the ranching and lumber industries and the Native American heritage. Check for free music and movie events during the summer. *Info: Downtown on Aspen between San Francisco and Leroux Streets. www. heritagesquaretrust.org.*

Those interested in the botany of the area will want to take a trip to the **Arboretum at Flagstaff**, located about seven miles south of Business I-40 via Woody Mountain Road. The collection includes mainly rare and endangered plant species, as well as one of the largest collections of high country wildflowers in America. Shaded walks, birds, a tranquil brook, fragrant butterfly garden and fantastic views of the San Francisco Peaks along a mile-long nature trail are some of the highlights. *Info: 4001 S. Woody Mountain Road. Tel. 928-774-1442. www.thearb.org. 9am-5pm April through October only. Closed Tuesdays. Admission $8.50 adults. $3 children 3-17.*

### Wupatki Loop

Some of the most fascinating attractions in the Flagstaff area aren't within the city limits, but on a loop route that covers a total of about 60 miles. The loop includes well-preserved Native American ruins and amazing volcanic formations.

Take US-89 12 miles north of Flagstaff and follow the signs to **Sunset Crater Volcano National Monument**. A massive volcanic eruption and extensive lava flow occurred here more than 900 years ago. Don't miss the **self-guided Bonito Lava Flow Trail** to experience the many different volcanic formations that remain a millennium after the 200-year long period of volcanic activity. The jagged black rocks stand out in stark contrast to the red, yellow and orange shades of a thousand-foot high cinder cone beyond.

Continue on the loop road for ten miles to the **Wupatki National Monument**, once home to the ancient native Anasazi and Sinagua civilizations. Along the way you'll see some excellent views of the **Painted Desert** in the distance. Park at the visitor's center to tour the largest complex in the park, the **Wupatki ruins**. A trail leads down to a group of five ruins as well as to an amphitheater used for ceremonial purposes and a ball court. Don't miss the blow-hole at the end of the trail. Native peoples believed this was where the earth breathed.

Other options in the park include the Lomaki Pueblo Trail, an easy half-mile walk, and the Wukoki, Citadel, and Nalakihu Pueblos, which are also reached by short quarter-mile trails. *Info: Off US-89 north of Flagstaff. Tel. 928-679-2365. www.nps.gov/wupa/index.htm. Open daily 9am-5pm. $20 per vehicle.*

### Walnut Canyon National Monument

If you haven't gotten enough of native cultures, you can add a side trip to Walnut Canyon on the way back to Flagstaff. This was home to an Indian culture known as the Sinagua. Here today are the remains of the community they developed between about 1125 and 1250 AD. You'll walk through impressive homes built beneath **overhanging cliffs** in the canyon's walls. The paved trail is steep, but worth the effort. *Info: 7.5 miles east of Flagstaff on I-40 (exit 204.) Tel. 928-526-3367. www.nps.gov/waca. Open daily 8am-5pm. $8 adults 17 and older.*

## WHERE TO STAY

### Inn at 410 $$

Winner of numerous awards, this B&B is located in a large two-story home a few short blocks from Flag's historic downtown district. The structure, built in 1907, is on a quiet street with nicely shaded grounds that include a small garden. Each room is decorated in a unique manner and features the southwestern décor of an earlier era. Breakfast is abundant, wholesome and delicious. *Info: www.inn410.com. Tel. 800-774-2008. Downtown: 410 N. Leroux Street. 9 rooms.*

**Little America Hotel  $$**
This classic lodge hotel is located on a magnificent 500-acre ponderosa forest with view of the San Francisco Mountains to the north. Guest accommodations are spread out in several buildings that go well with the natural surroundings. The rooms are unusually large. A large swimming pool and play area, along with the woods, make it a fun place for kids. There are hiking trails and a gym, along with three restaurants. *Info: www.littleamerica.com/flagstaff. Tel. 800-865- 1401. East of downtown: 2515 East Butler Ave. 247 rooms.*

### Hotel Monte Vista $
If you want to experience historic Flagstaff, the Monte Vista, in the heart of downtown, is for you. Over a hundred movies were filmed in and around Northern Arizona during the '40s and '50s and many Hollywood stars spent time here. Some of the rooms are named after these famous visitors. *Info: www.hotelmontevista.com. Tel. 800-545-3068. Downtown: 100 N. San Francisco St. 48 rooms.*

## WHERE TO EAT
### Brix $$$
Located a few blocks from the square, Brix offers contemporary cuisine in a comfy bungalow. The patio in back is especially nice in the summer. Excellent cheese plates and a wide variety of wines complement the menu, much of which is locally sourced. A fun place for cocktails as well. *Info: Tel. 928-213-1021. Downtown: 413 N. San Francisco. Open for dinner 7 nights a week. Reservations recommended.*

### Josephine's $$$
Great modern American food and wine served in a historic Craftsman bungalow. Far better food than you would expect out of a crunchy college

town. Delightful outdoor seating in summer and two indoor fireplaces for winter. Wine Spectator award of excellence winner. *Info: Tel. 928-779-3400. Downtown: 503 N. Humphrey's Street. Open daily in summer; closed Sunday rest of year. Reservations recommended.*

### The Cottage Place  $$$

A long-time favorite and excellent choice for continental cuisine, wine and atmosphere. Great tasting menu on weekends. One of the most formal places in town. Wine Spectator award of excellence winner. *Info: Tel. 928-774-8431. Two blocks south of downtown off Beaver: 126 West Cottage Avenue. Open for dinner Tuesday-Sunday. Reservations recommended.*

---

## Flagstaff Cheap Eats

These are both pretty close to campus and favorites with the college crowd:

- **Alpine Pizza** - Extremely casual with pool table and TVs. *(Tel. 928-779-4109. 7 N Leroux St.)*
- **Bun Huggers** – Burgers and shakes for the morning after. *(Tel. 928-779-3743. 901 S Milton Rd # A1.)*

---

### Mountain Oasis $-$$

Located right across the street from Heritage Square, Mountain Oasis would probably get a bunch of business just because of its location even if the food were mediocre. Luckily for Flagstaff diners, the food is very good. Featuring healthy cuisine from across the globe, Mountain Oasis is a great spot for lunch or dinner. The salads, sandwiches and smoothies are all delicious, as are the larger dinner entrees. Live music some evenings. *Info: Tel. 928-214-9270. Downtown: 11 East Aspen Ave. Open daily 11am-9pm.*

### Diablo Burger $

Gourmet burgers made with love and locally-sourced ingredients. Located in a tiny spot on the square, Diablo generally has a line and it's always worth the wait. Delicious fries, grilled cheese, and veggie burgers round out the menu. Just go. You will love it. *Info: Tel. 928-774-3274. Downtown: 120 N Leroux. Open for lunch and dinner Monday-Saturday.*

### La Bellavia $

The entire menu is a winner, but breakfast is especially popular. Don't miss the Swedish oat pancakes. If you like sausage, the chorizo scramble will put you over the top. *Info: Tel. 928-774-8301. Two blocks south of downtown on Beaver. 18 S Beaver St. Open for breakfast and lunch daily.*

### Macy's European Coffee House $

A coffee house, bakery and vegetarian restaurant, Macy's pretty much sums up the Flagstaff vibe. Definitely worth a visit. *Info: Tel. 928-774-2243. Two blocks south of downtown on Beaver. 14 S Beaver St, Flagstaff. Open Daily 6am-8pm (10pm Thurs-Sat.).*

### Salsa Brava $

My family's choice for the best Mexican food in town. The salsas are made from scratch daily, as are the rest of the menu items. Don't miss the Maui tacos or the carnitas. *Info: Tel. 928-779-5293. On the east side of town on Route 66. 2220 E Route 66. Open for lunch and dinner daily.*

### Beaver Street Brewery $

Great micro-brews, fun atmosphere, and hearty burgers and pizza. Delicious and appropriate for all ages. Nice outdoor seating. *Info: Tel. 928-779-0079. Two blocks south of downtown on Beaver: 11 S. Beaver St., No. 1.*

## Beef Jerky & Heineken

For an example of why we love Flagstaff, check out the **Pay-n-Take** (*Tel. 928-226-8595, 12 W. Aspen Ave.*) Where else can you find a convenience store with a full bar? Draft and bottled beer, wine by the bottle or glass, and your standard convenience store inventory. Good place to watch sporting events too.

## SHOPPING

There are many interesting specialty shops and galleries in downtown Flagstaff, most of these centered around Aspen Avenue and San Francisco Street. The **Museum of Northern Arizona** has a well-stocked museum gift shop with outstanding Native American crafts as well as an extensive bookstore. Then there is always the **Flagstaff Mall** (*www.flagstaffmall.com*) out Highway 89 East.

## NIGHTLIFE & ENTERTAINMENT

Because Flagstaff is a college town, there are plenty of bars and breweries that offer live music. All you have to do is wander through the downtown historic district or along Beaver Street by campus and you'll find a happening spot. The **Beaver Street Brewery**, **Lumberyard Brewery** and **Flagstaff Brewing Company** are always popular in the area. More mature tipplers might prefer **Cuvee 928** on Heritage Square or **FLG Terroir** at 17 N San Francisco St. The **Museum Club** at 3404 East Route 66 is THE place for honky-tonkin' to live music.

Cultural events in Flagstaff are held in the 200-seat amphitheater of the **Coconino Center for the Arts** (*Tel. 928-779-6921, www.culturalpartners. org*). The **Flagstaff Symphony Orchestra** is also active (*Tel. 928-774-5107, www.flagstaffsymphony.org*). The restored **Orpheum Theater** downtown (*Tel. 928-556-1580, www.orpheumpresents.com*) is a great place to catch national touring acts. **Theatrikos Theater Company** (*Tel. 928-774-1662, www.theatrikos.com*) offers high-quality community theater productions.

Summer is a wonderful time in Flagstaff, with weekly free concerts on the square and in the park, salsa dancing on the square, and movie nights. Check the schedule at *www.heritagesquaretrust.org*.

## SPORTS & RECREATION

**Northern Arizona University** has a full roster of NCAA sports in the Big Sky Conference. Check the local paper or *www.nauathletics.com* for ticket Information and schedules.

### Golf

There are some very nice golf courses that take advantage of the wonderful scenery in this part of the state. If you've never played at a higher altitude before, you'll love seeing your ball soar through the thinner mountain air. The only public course in Flagstaff is the **Elden Hills Golf Club** (*Tel. 928-527-7997*).

### Hiking & Extreme Fun

For great **area hikes**, see pages 76-77. Looking for an adrenaline rush? Visit the adventure ropes course at **Flagstaff Extreme**. Located just south of downtown at Fort Tuthill County Park, Flagstaff Extreme is an elevated ropes course winding through the pines. Four circuits, as well as a kids course, feature obstacles like hanging nets, suspended bridges, and ziplines that vary in difficulty and height. Booking in advance highly recommended. *Info: Fort Tuthill Loop Road, Tel. 888-259-0125. www.flagstaffexteme.com. 9am-3:30pm. $25 ages 7-11; $45 12 and above.*

### Biking
There are mountain biking trails galore in Flagstaff. Beginners will enjoy the gravel **FUTS** (Flagstaff Urban Trails System) that has trails all over town. More experienced bikers can make their way directly to the Elden Trail System north of town, to find miles of excellent single track. You can rent bikes at **Absolute Bikes** (*Tel. 928-779-5969, 202 E. US 66*).

### Horseback Riding
If you'd like to spend some time in the saddle, there are plenty of options. Try **Hartman Outfitters** (*www.hartmanoutfitters.com*) just out of town or **High Mountain Stables** (*highmountaintrailrides.com*), about 30 minutes away at Mormon Lake.

### Snow Sports
Flagstaff is the place to go for wintertime fun. For downhill skiing and snowboarding **Arizona Snowbowl** (*www.arizonasnowbowl.com*) offers 40 runs off of six lifts. Cross-country skiers will enjoy the wonderful **Flagstaff Nordic Center** (*www.flagstaffnordiccenter.com*), while sledders should hit **Wing Mountain Snow Play** area (*www.snowplayaz.com*).

# SEDONA & OAK CREEK CANYON
**Sedona**, with its surreal red rocks, mild year-round climate, and new-age "vortex sites" is the perfect place to play outside all day and then dine and sleep in luxury. An artist's colony in the '50s and '60s, Sedona now also draws hoards of nature lovers, spiritual seekers, and vacationing tourists.

## SEEING THE SIGHTS
Heading south from Flagstaff, be sure to take AZ-89A instead of I-17.

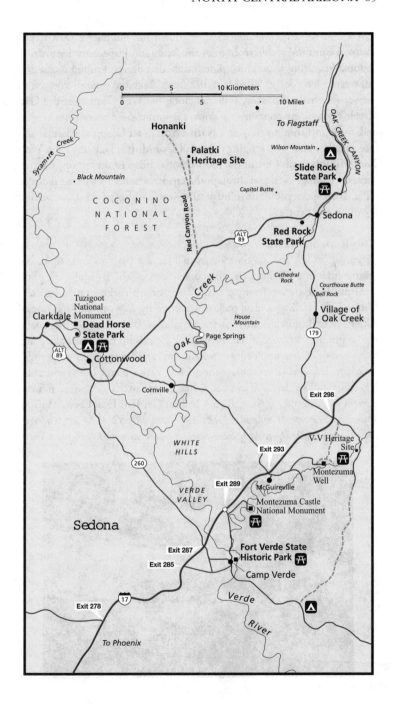

89A winds for a memorable 25 miles down the impressive **Oak Creek Canyon** from the southern edge of the Colorado Plateau to the town of Sedona. Featuring sheer cliffs, pine forests that descend to red rocks, and impressive deep gorges, it's a fantastic drive. Take the time to safely view the scenery from the many pullouts along the way. Don't miss the **Oak Creek Vista point** on your way down for impressive views of the canyon and an opportunity to shop at a **Native American Co-op market**. If you like to hike, plan on stopping 17.5 miles south of Flagstaff at the **West Fork Hiking Trail**. One of the most popular hikes in the region, the trail meanders along, over, and through the creek sheltered by soaring red rock cliffs. Wear shoes you don't mind getting wet (parking pass $10 per vehicle for up to five people).

### Slide Rock State Park

As you approach Sedona on 89-A, you'll see the park on your right. No matter how hot it is outside, the cool waters of the natural park pools at **Slide Rock** are a refreshing treat. The smooth rock water slides are a hit for kids of all ages. The park was named by *Life Magazine* as one of American's 10 most beautiful swimming holes. Be sure to get there early in the summer, because when the parking lot fills up they don't allow any more people. When apples are in season you can pick them from the park's orchard. This is also great place for picnic: Pack a picnic lunch when you leave Flagstaff so that you can eat al fresco here after your swim. You can also pick up supplies at the delicious **Indian Gardens Oak Creek Market**. *Info: 7 miles north of Sedona on AZ-89A. Tel. 928-282-3034. azstateparks. com/Parks/SLRO. Open daily 8am-5pm. (7pm in summer). $20 per vehicle.*

**Downtown Sedona**

Shoppers will be thrilled with the options in Sedona. Try **Main Street** for more commercial items like t-shirts and Native America curios, or the delightful shops of **Tlaquepaque** for art galleries and boutiques. Tlaquepaque, created as an "arts & crafts village," was designed to look like a Mexican pueblo. With pleasant courtyards, trickling fountains, and cobblestone pathways, it's a Sedona landmark. *Info: Located on 179 just south of the "Y." Tel. 928-282-4838. Open daily 10am-5pm.*

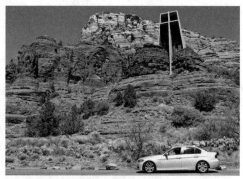

Continuing a few miles south on 179, you'll see the **Chapel of the Holy Cross**. Built between two huge sandstone peaks, the chapel offers splendid panoramic views. Even if you don't have a religious bone in your body, you're sure to be moved by the privileged view from this locale. *Info: Located on Chapel Road off of AZ 179 three miles south of the "Y." Tel. 928-282-4069. Open daily 9am-5pm (10am Sundays). No admission fee but donations accepted.*

Whether you hike, bike, jeep, or just drive, you've got to spend some time exploring the **red rocks** that make Sedona so unique. One of my favorite hikes for visitors is accessed by heading south on 179 towards the Village of Oak Creek to **Bell Rock**. You can simply walk out and climb around on the mesmerizing Bell Rock (easy option), or enjoy the mostly-level five-mile loop hike around stunning Bell Rock and Courthouse Buttes. Look for

the appropriately named Spaceship Rock on the backside of the loop. Bell Rock is a vortex site. *Info: 6.4 miles south of the 89/179 "Y" on 179. The trailhead and parking will be on your left. $5 Red Rock Pass required. You can buy passes at the trailhead or any of the Visitor's Centers.*

Other memorable Sedona hikes are: **Boyton Canyon**; **Airport Mesa**; and **Devil's Bridge**.

If hiking isn't your thing, you should drive the Red Rock Loop west of town on 89A for spectacular views. You'll see the surreal formations of **Red Rock State Park** as well as the magnificent hoodoos and spires of Cathedral Rocks. (Cathedral Rocks is supposed to be one of the most photographed spots in the US.) *Info: The paved Red Rock Loop Road is located west of Sedona off of 89A. If you wish to enter Red Rock State Park there is a $7 per adult and $4 per youth entry fee.*

While Sedona is known for its outdoor pursuits, it's also a mecca for spa-goers. The new-age flute music that accompanies most massages in the world somehow seems especially appropriate in Sedona. The **Enchantment Resort's Mii Amo Spa** is justifiably world famous, while **Adobe Grand Village** and **Sedona Rouge** also offer a full menu of spa treatments (*see Where to Sleep, below*).

## Experience the Vortex!

You won't be in Sedona long before you read or hear about **vortex sites**. The sites are apparently places where one can experience a concentration of swirling, uplifting energy. The **twisted juniper trees** found at many of the sites are offered as evidence of the strong energetic fields. You can take them with a grain of salt or seek them out, but either way, they're an integral part of Sedona.

## WHERE TO STAY

**Enchantment Resort $$$**
This beautiful resort is located at the end of a lovely secluded canyon. The hotel is enveloped by and blends in with the natural red rock formations that have made Sedona famous. Spread out in small Santa-Fe style buildings throughout the grounds, the large, comfortable guestrooms are either individual suites or more elaborate casitas.

Many have fireplaces and patios with unparalleled views. The resort offers a host of recreational opportunities including five swimming pools, a pitch & putt course, croquet and tennis. In addition, there are multiple guided activities each day such as bird walks, hikes, natural history lectures, meditation, yoga, mountain biking, and even gourd decoration. A meal at one of the restaurants is a good way to visit the property if you aren't staying here. The award-winning Mii Amo Spa draws visitors from around the world to enjoy the long list of available treatments. Located in a large building with its own pools and restaurant, the spa is definitely a destination in itself. The kids club, Camp Coyote, offers great programs for kids ages 4-12. *Info: www.enchantmentresort.com. Tel. 800-826-4180. West of Sedona in Boyton Canyon: 525 Boyton Canyon Road. 162 rooms.*

**L'Auberge de Sedona $$$**
Luxury and seclusion are the hallmarks of this hotel, a French country lodge

and cabins located along the banks of Oak Creek in a setting of dramatic natural beauty. You are conveniently located right in the heart of town, but you feel miles away once you drop down to the property. The gorgeous natural landscape will captivate you. All the guestrooms are large and beautifully furnished. Two gourmet restaurants are a treat in themselves, as is the indoor/outdoor wine bar. The heated pool and hot tub are great spots to soak in the views and the spa a wonderful place to be pampered. *Info: www.lauberge.com. Tel. 800-272-6777.*

### Sedona Rouge $$

The hip entry in the Sedona hotel market, the décor of the Sedona Rouge conjures up images of the Mediterranean and North Africa. Converting a standard motel into a chic destination is not easy, but these guys have pulled it off. Rooms feature flatscreen TVs and wireless internet. Full range of spa treatments available. Excellent dining at Reds. *Info: www.sedonarouge. com. Tel. 866-312-4111. West of downtown: 2250 West Hwy 89A. 77 rooms.*

### Sky Ranch Lodge $$

A great value, this motel-style property is located away from the hustle and bustle of town atop a mesa that affords spectacular views. Brilliant by sun-filled day, the view takes on a special warmth in the evening as the lights of Sedona twinkle in the fading daylight. Both the grounds and the rooms are spacious and comfortable. Some rooms include kitchenettes. Pool and hot tub. *Info: www.skyranchlodge.com. Tel. 888-708-6400. In town near the airport: Top of Airport Road. 94 rooms.*

### Days Inn Kokopelli Sedona $

A nice value in the moderately priced category, the Days Inn Kokopelli is attractive and comfortable. Sporting red rock views, the hotel offers free wifi, free parking, free breakfast, and a pool. Located in the Village of Oak Creek out of the hubbub of Sedona, the hotel is a great launching pad for adventures around Bell Rock. *Info: www.daysinn.com. Tel. 928-284-1100. Five miles south of downtown in the Village of Oak Creek. 6465 Arizona 179. 42 rooms.*

## WHERE TO EAT

### L'Auberge Restaurant at L'Auberge de Sedona $$$

This romantic spot, tucked in near the gurgling Oak Creek, is pretty much the epitome of perfection. With impeccable French cuisine and service,

L'Auberge really treats you like royalty. The patio just might be the most exquisite spot in Sedona. If you can't afford dinner, try the wonderful breakfast here. Dress pants and collared shirts for men. *Info: Tel. 928-282-1667. Downtown: 301 L'Auberge Lane. Open daily for breakfast, lunch, and dinner. Dinner reservations recommended.*

## Elote Café $$$

Located inside the Kings Ransom Sedona Hotel, the Elote Café is the epitome of upscale Mexican dining. Every dish is delicious. If you are in town one of the nights it is open, you should definitely dine here. The lamb is so tender it almost falls apart at the touch of your fork. You can't go wrong with any dish, which simply means that you will want to come back for more. The views here are wonderful as well, but you'll mostly be paying attention to the outstanding food. *Info: Tel. 928-203-0105. Kings Ransom Sedona Hotel. 771 Highway 179. Open Tuesday-Saturday for dinner only. Reservations recommended.*

## View 180 at Enchantment Resort $$

Given the amazing views of Boynton Canyon offered here, the restaurant would be packed regardless of the quality of food. They take it a step further though and offer a wide variety of specialty cocktails along with an intriguing menu of tapas. *Info: Tel. 928-204-6000. North of town: 525 Boynton Canyon Rd. Open daily for breakfast, lunch, and dinner. Dinner reservations recommended.*

## El Rincon Restaurante Mexicano $$

Featuring Mexican cuisine with a bit of Navajo influence, El Rincon has been a Sedona standard for 30 years. Located in the pleasant "village" of Tlaquepaque, El Rincon's décor fits right in. The adobe building features tile and iron work from Mexico. Try the Navajo pizzas if you aren't going to make it up to the Navajo Nation. *Info: Tel. 928-282-4648. Located just south of the Y on Hwy. 179 at The Bridge. Open daily 11am-9pm (8pm on Sundays.) Dinner reservations recommended.*

## Reds Bistro at Sedona Rouge $$

Stylish and chic, Reds manages to pull off being comfortable at the same time. The food, haute takes on many American favorites, is absolutely delicious. Enjoy the upscale atmosphere of the dining room, or just relax in the *Info: Tel. 928-203-4111. West of downtown: 2250 West Hwy 89A. Open daily breakfast, lunch, and dinner daily.*

**Mesa Grill Sedona at the Airport  $$**
Yes, eating at the airport is a little random, but in Sedona it means great views and good food at the same time. This southwest-style grill offers quality food in a memorable setting. *Info: Tel. 928-282- 2400. In town at the airport: 1185 Airport Rd. Open daily 7am-9pm.*

**Desert Flour Bakery & Bistro  $**
Stop in for sinfully delicious pastries, or grab one of their excellent made-to-order sandwiches. You can eat in, or take your food along for a picnic. The salads here are also outstanding. *Info: Tel. 928-284-4633. South of downtown in the Village of Oak Creek. 6446 Highway 179. Open 7am-3pm Monday, Tuesday. 7am-8:30pm Wednesday-Saturday. 8am-2pm Sundays.*

**Indian Gardens Oak Creek Market  $**
A café, market, coffee shop, and liquor store all in one, Indian Gardens is a treat no matter what mood strikes you. Enjoy hearty breakfasts and sandwiches or pick up artisanal beer, wine and local produce. *Info: Tel. 928-282-7702. Northeast of downtown in Oak Creek Canyon. 3951 N State Route 89A. 8am-6pm.*

## SHOPPING
Sedona is full of shopping opportunities. There are galleries and shops along **89A** on the main drag of town as well as at the **Tlaquepaque Village** on 179 right before the Y. Another series of galleries lines Highway 179 between Sedona and the Village of Oak Creek – see several at once at **Hozho Plaza**. For discounts, try the **Factory Outlet Stores** on 179 at the Village of Oak Creek.

## NIGHTLIFE & ENTERTAINMENT
The Sedona nightlife concentrates in bars and brewpubs in the heart of town. The **Oak Creek Brewing Company** (*Tel. 928-204-1300*) has live music on weekends. The **Sedona Arts Center** (*www.sedonaartscenter.com*) hosts various cultural events.

## SPORTS & RECREATION
### Golf
Sedona has a number of good courses, but the **Sedona Golf Resort** (*Tel. 800-426-6148*) is especially beautiful. The par 3 hole #10 stands out as one of the most photographed holes in Arizona.

## Hiking

Sedona has more wonderful trails than there is space to mention here. Located in the **Red Rock District** of the **Coconino National Forest** (*www. fs.usda.gov/coconino*), the town boasts great hiking in every direction. The Courthouse Loop, moderate, located between Sedona and the Village of Oak Creek, is one of my favorites for first-time visitors. Boyton Canyon, an easy hike along a vortex site, is also very popular. The Devil's Bridge trail, moderate, leads to the largest sandstone arch in the Sedona area.

## Biking

Although not as famous for biking as the slick rock of Moab, Sedona has some of its own sick slick rock. Advanced riders will love the Broken Arrow Loop, between the Village of Oak Creek and Sedona, while beginners should enjoy the easy Bell Rock Pathway in the same area. Rentals at **Absolute Bikes** (*Tel. 877-284-1242, 6101 Highway 179 in the Village of Oak Creek*).

## Horseback Riding

You can go with **Trail Horse Adventures** to see the red rocks from the back of a horse (*www.trailhorseadventures.com*).

## Jeep Tours

Probably the most popular Sedona adventure, jeep tours are easy to arrange and fun to take. Check out the original operator, **Pink Jeep Tours** (*www. pinkjeep.com, Tel. 800-873-3662*), or the supposedly more eco-conscious Hummer tours with **Sedona Off Road Adventures** (*www.sedonajeeptours. com, Tel. 928-282-6656*).

## Hot Air Balloon Tours

Imagine skimming over the red rocks of Sedona on a silent morning in a floating balloon. This experience is yours for the having with Northern

**Lights Balloon Expeditions**, (*Tel. 800 230-6222, www.northernlightballoon.com*).

# COTTONWOOD, JEROME & PRESCOTT

Wineries, shopping, historic mining towns, wonderful natural scenery, and real cowboy culture can all be discovered and enjoyed in this part of the state. If you have time it is definitely worth taking a couple of days to explore this area.

### Cottonwood

The wine industry in Arizona has taken off like a climbing vine, and nowhere is that more apparent than in **Cottonwood**. What was once a sleepy little town for retirees has transformed itself into a compelling destination with boutique shopping, first-class dining, and a profusion of wineries and tasting rooms. If you have not been to Cottonwood in the last year or so, you owe it another visit.

Located just 19 miles southwest of Sedona, Cottonwood merits at least a few hours if not a day or two depending on your interest in viticulture and enology. The action in Cottonwood centers around **Old Town** along Main Street. Here you can pop your head into numerous shops that sell everything from high-end foodstuffs and clothing to Mexican curios to locally made art. This is also where the majority of the town's unusually high proportion of excellent restaurants are located.

The main draw to Cottonwood and the surrounding area however is the profusion of wineries and tasting rooms. You can learn all about the **Verde Valley Wine Trail**, as it has been dubbed, at *www.vvwinetrail.com*. There are four tasting rooms located **along Main Street** in Cottonwood. These include **Fire Mountain Wines, Pillsbury Wine Company**, and my two in-town favorites – **Burning Tree Cellars** and **Arizona Stronghold**. It is also worth a drive to **Clarkdale** to do some sipping at **Four Eight Wineworks**, an incubator co-op with a continually changing line-up.

To really get a sense of the area's passion for all things grape, grab a designated driver and hit the road around Cottonwood. On-site wineries that merit a visit include **Chateau Tumbleweed**, with its irreverent attitude but serious wine; **Javelina Leap** with a grassy outdoor area and saloon-style tasting room; and **Alcantara Vineyards**.

The "elder statesman" of the group and the one winery that is a must-visit is **Page Spring Cellars** in **Cornville** (between Sedona and Cottonwood). Located on the banks of Oak Creek, Page Springs is a step ahead of the others in terms of tenure and amenities. Excellent food accompanies the various flights of wine. Here you can also book a massage on the banks of the creek or even try some downward dog. bocce ball and corn hole make it an easy place to while away the day.

If you want to counteract some of that wine tasting with some exercise, there are great options in the area.

**Dead Horse Ranch State Park** is just two miles from Old Town off of North 10th St. The park's **Verde River** is one of the Arizona desert's last free-flowing rivers. It sustains a large regional wildlife population and a lush riparian community in the dense forest along its banks. Visitors enjoy strolling along the river or around the small lakes, bird watching, canoeing, picnicking, fishing, or just sticking their feet in the cool water. (Don't worry, there are no dead horses there now. When the owners bought the place in the '40s there was a dead horse by the road. The kids in the family kept calling it the Dead Horse Ranch and the name stuck.) Try the **Lime Kiln Trail** if you are interested in a hike. *Info: 675 Dead Horse Ranch Road off of North 10th St. in Cottonwood. Tel. 928-634-5283. azstateparks.com/ Parks/DEHO. Open daily. $7 per vehicle.*

With swimming holes, red-rock views, and a mostly level trail along a lovely flowing creek, the **Parson's Trail** in the **Sycamore Canyon Wilderness** between Cottonwood and Clarkdale is a stand-out hiking trail in the state (see the Coconino National Forest website for more details: *www.fs.usda. gov/coconino*).

If kayaking down the **Verde River** floats your boat, try either **Clarkdale Kayak** (*clarkdalekayak.com*) or **CenterFocus Adventures** (*thecenterfocus. com*). CenterFocus also offer stand-up paddleboard rides down the Verde as well as rock climbing and guided hikes.

If Native American ruins are more your speed, don't miss the **Tuzigoot National Monument** located just out of town towards Clarkdale. Meaning "crooked water" in Apache, Tuzigoot is what remains of a 12th century Sinaguan village constructed atop a ridge that rises above the Verde Valley. An easy trail leads to the visitor's center and loops around the ruins. You can climb up to the top to get a good view of the entire ruins and the Verde Valley beyond. *Info: Off AZ289 near Clarkdale. Tel. 928-634-5564. www. nps.gov/tuzi/index.htm. Open 8am-4pm daily. $10 per person over 15.*

Both train buffs and nature enthusiasts will want to head 2.5 miles from Old Town Cottonwood to Clarkdale, as it's the starting point for a scenic ride on the **Verde Canyon Railroad.** By taking the train you are able to traverse a portion of the Sycamore Wilderness that is not accessible by road. The trip takes about four hours and includes several deep canyon trestle crossings. You can see wildlife including deer and bald eagles, as well as the remains of many Sinaguan villages. The train features open and closed cars and there is food service on board. *Info: Tel. 800-320-0718. www. verdecanyonrr.com. Contact the railroad for departure times. One or two trains depart daily depending on demand. $65 Adult (coach), $45 child (coach.) First class seating also available.*

## WHERE TO SLEEP & EAT
### Iron Horse Inn $$
With a perfect location right on Main Street, the Iron Horse Inn is a comfortable oasis when you feel that post-tasting afternoon nap coming on.

This one-time motor court motel has been transformed into lovely place to stay in Cottonwood. Located around a pleasant central courtyard, all the rooms feature pillow top mattresses, flat screen TVs, microwaves and mini-fridges. A small hospitality room includes fresh fruit and coffee. *Info: www.ironhorseoldtown.com. Tel. 928-634-8031. 1034 N Main St.*

### The Tavern Hotel $$

This ten-room boutique hotel located on Main St. also offers two cottages. With a cosmopolitan up-town feel, the hotel meets demanding standards. Very comfortable rooms await guests after a day of sippin' or shoppin'. Sister restaurant The Tavern Grille offers guests a free drink upon arrival. *Info: www.thetavernhotel.com. Tel 928-639-1669. 904 N Main St.*

### Abbie's Kitchen $$$

Located in a small cottage a few blocks from the main commercial cluster of Main Street, Abbie's is a wonderful surprise of fine dining in this small town. It's no wonder after you learn that chef Abbie Ashford has cooked for both royalty and celebs. Classic dishes like duck breast and filet minion share the menu with spicy sugar bacon twists and a mushroom goat cheese purse, all dubbed "high-end comfort food." *Info: www.abbieskitchen.com. Tel. 928-634-3400. 778 N Main St. Open Wed-Sat for dinner. Reservations recommended.*

### Pizzaria BOCCE Patio Bar $$

This welcoming vibe of this slick modern restaurant, with plentiful outdoor seating and a namesake bocce ball court, extends to the service as well. The highlight however is the food – wood-fired Naples-style pizza that will beckon you back time and time again. *Info: boccecottonwood.com. Tel. 928-202-3597. 1060 N. Main St. Dinner Monday-Friday. Lunch and dinner Sat. Lunch only Sun.*

### The Tavern Grill $$

If it's classic pub food you crave, this is the spot for it in Cottonwood. Big juicy burgers, yummy fries, and even salads for that friend on a diet. A full bar and large TVs make it a fun spot to hang out for a game. *Info: http://thetaverngrille.com. Tel. 928-634-6669. 914 N Main St. Open daily 11am-9pm.*

There are no lack of great breakfast and lunch spots on Main Street in Cottonwood. Two favorites are **Crema Café** (*917 N. Main*) and the **Old**

**Rooster Café** (*901 N. Main)*, offering excellent food and patio seating. For dessert or a small savory bite, don't miss **Paradise Point Café** (*1092 N. Main)*.

## Jerome

Perched high on Mingus Mountain about eight miles above Cottonwood is the charming town of **Jerome**. This enjoyable burgh, once a booming city, boasted a population of 15,000 and was known as the Wickedest Town of the West at the height of its copper mining days. With the closure of the last mine in the 1950s, Jerome almost became a ghost town. It has enjoyed a rebirth of late however and is home to a number of art galleries, wineries, shops and restaurants to serve the growing visitor population. The streets of the picturesque town wind up and down Cleopatra Hill, and its buildings, many constructed in the late 1800s, seem to perch precariously on the brink.

My favorite thing to do in Jerome is simply walk the streets, taste some wine, enjoy the views, and then have a nice, long lunch or dinner at one of Jerome's yummy restaurants (see *Where to Sleep and Eat Jerome*).

There are four **wineries** in Jerome. The most famous of these, **Caduceus Cellars** (*158 Main St*), is owned by musician Maynard James Keenan. He has been -- and continues to be -- a central figure in developing winemaking in the Verde Valley. His tasting room is definitely worth a stop. The three others, all located along Hull Ave, are **Cellar 433**, **Passion Cellars**, and **Echo Canyon Winery**.

If you've still got some touring in you, the **Douglas Mansion** at the **Jerome State Historic Park** is worth a visit. One of the most interesting features of the museum is a large three-dimensional model of the town as it appeared in its heyday, including a cutaway of the mines. *Info: Just off 89A in Jerome. Tel. 928-634-5381. azstateparks.com/Parks/JERO. Open daily 8am-5pm. $7 adults. $4 children 7-13.*

If you end up in Jerome in the evening, I would suggest spending the night so that you can enjoy the lovely drive down to Prescott during the light of day.

## WHERE TO STAY & EAT

### Jerome Grand Hotel $$

Located in a historic five-story Spanish mission structure, the Jerome

Grand Hotel perches at the top of town. The beautifully restored rooms offer fantastic views. If you enjoy hotels with character, this is the place for you. Don't miss the excellent Asylum restaurant as well. *Info: www.jeromegrandhotel.net. Tel. 888-817-6788. 200 Hill St.*

### The Asylum at the Jerome Grand Hotel $$$

Have a drink on the patio and enjoy the views before making your way inside to a wonderful dining experience. Start with the squash soup and you won't be disappointed. Wine Spectator Award of Excellence winner. *Info: Tel. 928-639-3197. Above town: 200 Hill St. Open daily for lunch and dinner.*

### Flatiron Café $$

Famous for killer breakfast burritos and bread pudding that is usually gone by noon, the Flatiron also serves up a memorable lunch. Located in a wedge of a building reminiscent of the Flatiron in New York City, the cozy little restaurant at the bottom of the hill offers both indoor and outdoor seating. *Info: Tel. 928-634-2733. Downtown: Flatiron Building I, 416 Main St. 8am-4pm. Closed Tuesdays and Wednesdays.*

### Haunted Hamburger $

If good food in a casual environment is what you're after, you'll find it here. Try the gourmet burgers on the outdoor deck and follow them up with the chocolate cake. *Info: Tel. 928-634-0554. Downtown: 410 N Clark Street.*

### Grapes Restaurant & Wine Bar $$

Offering stellar views and delicious food, Grapes is a welcome entrant to the Jerome eating scene. The salads are crisp and delicious, the pizzas crunchy and tasty, and the wine top-notch. With pasta, sandwiches, pizza (including gluten free), and more, Grapes will please everybody in your bunch. *Info: www.grapesjerome.com. 111 Main St. Tel. 928-639-8477. Open daily lunch and dinner.*

## Prescott

**Prescott**, 35 miles past Jerome on AZ-89A, began as a mining town in the middle of the 19th century. Retirees and vacationers flock here now for the mild weather and small-town feel. Prescott embraces its cowboy history, which you'll see in many of the area attractions.

Begin your tour of Prescott's downtown at the lovely tree-covered **Courthouse Plaza**, the center of civic life. Both visitors and locals set up blankets

under the huge shade trees and enjoy the many fairs here on the weekends. There are several statues on the grounds, including impressive **Bucky O'Neill Monument**, which honors the first volunteer in the Spanish-American War and the man who founded the Rough Riders of Teddy Roosevelt fame.

Near the Courthouse and along Gurley St. you'll find the historic portion of town. Prescott has over 500 buildings listed in the National Register of Historic Places, which is more than any other community in the state. The greatest concentration of shops, especially antique dealers, is located along a two-block stretch of Cortez St., north of Courthouse Plaza. **Whiskey Row,** located off the plaza on the 100 block of Montezuma Street, was where the miners came to let off a little steam. Locals and tourists do the same nowadays in the many **cowboy saloons** on this stretch. (There are ice cream shops and art galleries here as well.) Most of the buildings were constructed between 1900-1905 after a fire wiped out the first version of Whiskey Row.

The **Sharlot Hall Museum**, on Gurley, consists of three historic buildings that are furnished in the manner similar to when they were first built. The **Governor's Mansion** is a highlight with an excellent display of western transportation that included a stagecoach and Conestoga wagon. *Info: 415 Gurley St. Tel. 928-445-3122. www.sharlot.org. Open daily 10am-4pm (5pm in summer.) Adults $9, $5 youth 13-17.*

The climate is what draws many people to Prescott. When it's smoking hot in Phoenix you can enjoy wonderful hikes and bike rides here. Be sure to spend some time exploring the great outdoors. (See *Sports & Recreation below.*)

### Cowboy Art
If you're a fan of cowboy art, the P**hippen Museum** seven miles north of Prescott on AZ-89, has a sizable collection of works by famous Western artists. *Info: Tel. 928-778-1385. www.phippenartmuseum.org.*

## WHERE TO STAY

**Hassayampa Inn  $$**
This historic property dates from 1927 and fits in perfectly with the surroundings of Court House Square and its old shops and buildings.
Exudes charm and comfort, although most of the rooms are on the small side. Try breakfast at the hotel's Peacock room. (The inn is purported to be haunted be a ghost named Faith.) *Info: www.hassayampainn.com. Tel. 800-322-1927. Downtown: 122 E Gurley St. 68 rooms.*

**Hotel Vendome  $$**
Located just a half-block from Courthouse Plaza, the Vendome offers modern comforts in a century-old building. The 20 rooms boast a variety of configurations and many have claw-foot tubs. Amenities include complimentary breakfast, free Wi-Fi, and a guest pantry. The hotel's Fremont Bar is a favorite gathering place. *Info: www.vendomehotel.com. Tel. 928-776-0900. Downtown: 230 S. Cortez St. 20 rooms.*

**The Motor Lodge  $**
Decorated with a plethora of retro touches, the Motor Lodge is a welcoming and friendly inn. From the complimentary beer or wine upon arrival to home-baked cookies, thick towels, and soft beds, the Motor Lodge is a traveler's delight. Three blocks from the town square. *Info: www.themotorlodge.com. Tel. 928-717-0157. Downtown: 503 S. Montezuma St. 12 rooms.*

**Hotel St. Michael  $**
Located right in the heart of Whiskey Row, the St. Michael is not for those who want tranquility. If you want to be a part of the action however, this is the place for you. The rooms are old-fashioned (i.e. on the small side), but you can inquire about a suite if you need more space. Breakfast at the wonderful Caffe St. Michael included. *Info: www.stmichaelhotel.com. Tel. 800-678-3757. Downtown: 205 W Gurley St. 72 rooms.*

## WHERE TO EAT

**Iron Springs Café  $$**
Housed in the historic depot building, the Iron Springs Café is definitely a local favorite. It's not right in the center of town, so few tourists wander

in, but it's very popular anyway. With Southwest and Cajun influences, dishes like the garlic shrimp tamales are fantastic. *Info: Tel. 928-443-8848. West of downtown: 1501 W. Iron Springs Rd.*

**Murphy's Restaurant $$**
Murphy's is located in a refurbished commercial building dating from the 1890s in the heart of Prescott's historic downtown. Good mesquite broiled meat dishes as well as wonderful home baked bread. They are also known for their huge selection of domestic and imported beers. *Info: Tel. 928-445-4044. Downtown: 201 North Cortez St. Lunch and dinner served daily. Sunday brunch.*

**Bin 239 $$**
This little wine-cafe is a great Prescott asset. Enjoy wonderful wood-fired pizza, fresh salads, and an extensive wine list. Desserts are primo as well. *Info: Tel. 928-445-3855. Downtown: 239 N. Marina St. Closed Sunday.*

**Dinner Bell $**
Although they have "dinner" in the name, this is the spot for breakfast. If you want hearty and lots of options, come here. *Info: Tel. 928-445-9888. Downtown: 321 W. Gurley St. Open for breakfast and lunch until 2pm daily.*

## NIGHTLIFE & ENTERTAINMENT
**Whiskey Row**, concentrated in the vicinity of Gurley and Montezuma Streets, is where you'll find the nightlife in Prescott. Check out **Matt's Saloon** and **The Palace**.

If you lean towards the fine arts, the **Prescott Fine Arts Association** (*Tel. 928-445-3286, www.pfaa.net*) stages plays, music and dance at its theater on Marina. Summer evenings see performances held on Courthouse Plaza (*www.visit-prescott.com/event-calendar.html*).

For gambling you can hit **Bucky's Casino** (*www.buckyscasino.com*) on the way into Prescott on Highway 69. Otherwise you'll have to do some driving to visit the **Cliff Castle Casino** (*Tel. 928-567-7900*) in Camp Verde at exit 289 off I-17.

## SPORTS & RECREATION
### Hiking
The gorgeous **Granite Basin Recreation Area**, out Iron Springs Road,

is a must for hikers and mountain bikers. The massive granite boulders, smoothed by weather and time, look like statues reflected in **Granite Basin Lake**. Enjoy loop hikes through the pines or out and backs.

Another fantastic granite outcropping can be found five miles north of town on AZ 89 at Granite Dells and lovely Watson Lake. It looks like a giant took some handfuls of marbles (i.e. smoothed boulders) and threw them all around the water. The **Peavine Trail** is a good one in this area.

One of Prescott's better-known natural features is a rugged granite outcropping known as the **Thumb Butte**. Take Gurley three miles out (it becomes Thumb Butte Road) and enjoy a two-mile loop hike up to through the Ponderosa pines to the base of the butte for great views of the **Prescott National Forest**.

### Golf
Many visitors take advantage of Prescott's mild climate by enjoying a round of golf. **Antelope Hills Golf Club** (*www.antelopehillsgolf.com*) offers two public courses.

# I-17 CORRIDOR
There are a few sights that don't fit neatly into one of the town descriptions, but are worth a stop if you are coming to or from Phoenix. The best of these is the impressive ruins at **Montezuma Castle National Monument** (*see photo on next page*). This cliff dwelling is an excellent example of Sinagua architecture. Built into the hollow of a vertical cliff, the five-story dwelling was constructed in the early part of the 12th century. Located along a pleasant creek, the site is well-worth a visit. *Info: Exit 289, three miles off Interstate 17. Tel. 928-567-3322. www.nps.gov/moca/index.htm. Open daily 8am-5pm. Admission $5 ages 16 and over.*

Closer to Phoenix, at the Cordes Junction turnoff to Prescott, is the unusual **Arcosanti**, the brainchild of recently-deceased architect Paolo Soleri. His vision includes a complete urban community for 5,000 totally in harmony with nature. Encompassing more than 4,000 acres of natural area, the 15-acre town-site is intended to be a community for working artists. It has been under construction for many years and will probably never be completed, but it remains an interesting place to visit. There is even lodging available if you really want to experience archeology first-hand. *Info: Off exit 262 on I-17. Follow signs for three miles down dirt road. Tel. 928-632-7135. Open*

**Pause for Pie**

No visit to Arizona would be complete without a stop at the **Rock Springs Café** for a slice of pie. Located at exit 242 between Anthem and Cordes Junction, Rock Springs is a state gem. Berry pies, cream pies, and even gooey Jack Daniels pecan pies are all there for the tasting.

*9am-5pm. Guided one-hour tours are offered every hour from 10am-4pm except at noon. $10 fee for tour.*

# 6. THE GRAND CANYON

## HIGHLIGHTS

- **South Rim, west section** – The Abyss Overlook; a meal at El Tovar; the Visitor's Center; bike ride along West Rim Drive

- **South Rim, east section** – Yaki, Moran, Lipan, and Desert View overlooks

- **North Rim** – Bright Angel Point, Cape Royal, Grand Canyon Lodge

- **Hiking into the Canyon** – but only if you're up for it physically

Any words used to describe the Grand Canyon are insufficient to do it proper justice. The same is true for pictures and video, because these mediums cannot capture the depth and layers you see when standing on the canyon's rim.

The **Grand Canyon National Park** covers 1900 square miles and is 277 miles long. The **Colorado River** divides the **North Rim** from the **South Rim**. Although it only averages about 15 miles across from one rim to the other, the canyon isn't traversed by any roads. So, if you have to travel by car from the South to North Rims it's a 210-mile drive. The **South Rim is much more accessible** from major population centers and is, therefore, the focus of much of this chapter.

## ORIENTATION

By car the South Rim is 84 miles from Flagstaff and 223 miles from Phoenix. Travelers coming from the east should take I-40 to Exit 195 in Flagstaff and then US 180 to the Grand Canyon. If you're coming on I-40 from the west, use Exit 165 in Williams and then go north on AZ 64 for about an hour to the canyon. From Phoenix take I-17 north until its end in Flagstaff and proceed as above via US 180.

## SEEING THE SIGHTS

Yes, it's just a big hole in the ground, but it's the most impressive and beautiful big hole you'll ever see. Even if all you have is one day, this is the single most important and majestic sight in Arizona, so make sure you take a gander while you're here.

### SOUTH RIM

The South Rim is sub-divided into the **West and East Rim Drives**, with the **Grand Canyon Village** separating the two. During the summer months

### Geology Lesson

The walls of the Grand Canyon are a veritable museum of natural history that span about one half of the earth's almost five billion year existence. The forces of erosion, primarily the cutting action of the Colorado River, but also wind and rain, have exposed many colorful layers of rock strata. The oldest of the 12 layers (about 1.7 billion years) is at the bottom and the youngest (only 250 million years) is at the top.

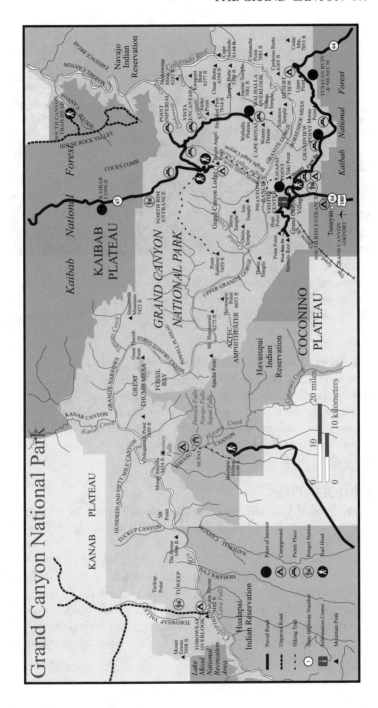

Any words used to describe the Grand Canyon are insufficient to do it proper justice. The same is true for pictures and video, because these mediums cannot capture the depth and layers you see when standing on the canyon's rim.

The **Grand Canyon National Park** covers 1900 square miles and is 277 miles long. The **Colorado River** divides the **North Rim** from the **South Rim**. Although it only averages about 15 miles across from one rim to the other, the canyon isn't traversed by any roads. So, if you have to travel by car from the South to North Rims it's a 210-mile drive. The **South Rim is much more accessible** from major population centers and is, therefore, the focus of much of this chapter.

## ORIENTATION

By car the South Rim is 84 miles from Flagstaff and 223 miles from Phoenix. Travelers coming from the east should take I-40 to Exit 195 in Flagstaff

### Use Minutes & Learn

If you've got a cell phone, you have a built-in tour guide. There are numerous points along the South Rim where you can listen to two-minute spiels on aspects of the canyon that range from geology to Native American history. Just look for the **Park Ranger Audio Tour** signs, *call 928-225-2907*, and enter the stop number.

the canyon's rim. It can make you feel very small and insignificant and does justice to the marvels of nature.

This is also where you will find the **South Rim Visitor Center** and **Canyon View Information Plaza**. It is worth a stop here to orient yourself and get information about ranger guided activities, shuttle bus routes, day hikes, bike rentals and routes, current weather, park information, and commercial trips and tours. You are also encouraged to park your car here and either bike, shuttle, or walk to the Grand Canyon Village.

A little further along the road is the turnoff to **Yavapai Point**, which is also home to the small **Yavapai Museum**. Walk through the museum, which focuses on the canyon's geology.

If you've got the time and the stamina, there is a trail that leads along the canyon rim from Mather Point to Hermit's Rest. This is the **only flat trail in the park**, so if you want to hike a little but can't handle steep inclines, this is the trail for you.

### Grand Canyon Village

After Yavapai Point you'll soon reach the **Grand Canyon Village area** which is where the majority of services, including hotels, are located. Be advised that it is among the most crowded portions of the park at any time. (Keep an eye out for elk on the road, especially at night.) It is also the location of another of the park's Visitor Centers, a good place to see some interesting exhibits on the park's natural and human history as well as to get information from the always helpful and friendly rangers. This is also where the shuttle service begins.

If you're not spending the night at one of the hotels on the rim, take some time now to walk along the rim trail in front of the village. Don't miss the **Kolb Studio**, built by two photographers early in the 1900s on the edge of the canyon rim. There are some great views out the studio window. It's also a good place to escape from the elements for a few minutes as it is nice and warm in the winter and cool in the summer.

If you are going to do any hiking into the canyon, one excellent option here is the **Bright Angel Trail** (*see photo on next page*). It is the same trail that is used by the mule trips. (By the way, mules always have the right of way should you encounter them on the trail.) The trail descends to the Colorado River by a series of steep switchbacks. It is not for the faint of heart,

although inexperienced hikers often enjoy going part of the way down just to get the feel of descending into the canyon. Be sure to take plenty of water.

Heed this warning for all canyon trails: **Never attempt to reach the Colorado River at the bottom of the canyon and try to get back in the same day.** People have died from exhaustion trying to do so.

Continuing along the eight-mile West Rim Drive you'll come to the Hopi, Maricopa, and Pima Points. They are all beautiful, but the best of the lot is the next overlook, called **The Abyss**. Here the **Great Mojave Wall** of the canyon has an almost sheer vertical drop of 3,000 feet. This provides visitors with a clear view of the **Tonto Platform** within the canyon and the **Colorado River**. The Abyss is the only place on the West Rim that the river can be seen. The West Rim ends at **Hermit's Rest**, which is the start of the 17-mile round-trip **Hermit Trail**. If you have chosen to ride a bike

## Reading Material

In 1869, one-armed **John Wesley Powell** and a small group journeyed a thousand miles on the Colorado River and through the entire Grand Canyon, exploring previously unknown lands. Read about it in Powell's excellent *Exploration of the Colorado River and Its Canyons*. Then, in the late 1800s, **Fred Harvey** began transporting visitors to the canyon. His adventurous employees are profiled in *The Harvey Girls: Women Who Opened the West*.

along the West Rim and are tired, this is a good spot to put your bike on the shuttle for the return trip.

## Sunrise, Sunset

Don't miss either sunrise or sunset in the park, as they are truly spectacular. The sunrises are best at Lipan, Mather, Yaki, and Yavapai Points, while the sunsets are most spectacular at Desert View, Hopi, Lipan, Mojave, and Pima Points.

### East Rim Drive

The **East Rim Drive** covers a one-way distance of 23 miles. The less traveled East Rim has its overlooks spaced further apart than the West Rim and most of them are reached by spur roads of about a mile in length. Many of the viewpoints on the East Rim afford more spectacular vistas than the West Rim, so don't miss them.

**Yaki Point** has some of the best canyon views of any overlook and is also the beginning of the **South Kaibab Trail**, which reaches **Phantom Ranch** and the river by a different route than the more popular Bright Angel Trail.

You'll want to stop at both **Moran** and **Lipan Points** for different perspectives than offered on the West Rim overlooks. You're looking back into the canyon more than down upon it. This affords a greater appreciation of the vastness of the canyon because you can see the different layers within it. You can also see how the gorge that contains the Colorado River is actually

a canyon within a canyon. The **Grandview Trail**, off Grandview Point on the East Rim, is an excellent day-hike as it doesn't go all the way to the bottom of the canyon. Instead, it leads to colorful **Horseshoe Mesa**. (This doesn't mean it isn't strenuous, however.)

The grand finale is the spectacular **Desert View** (*see photo on previous page*). From this point you can see a truly spectacular panorama that includes, besides the canyon itself, the **Colorado River**, colorful **Vermilion Cliffs**, the distant **San Francisco Peaks**, and a portion of the **Painted Desert**. A re-creation of an Anasazi tower, called the **Watchtower**, was built here early in the 1900s. You can climb up top for even better views.

### Mule Trips & Tours
People have been **riding mules to the bottom** of the Grand Canyon for more than 100 years. Mules are preferable to horses because they are more sure-footed and have a much better temperament for the task. Be aware though that you will be spending a lot of time in the saddle. This is a very popular way to see the canyon, so it is suggested that **reservations be made six to eight months in advance**. (*See Sports & Recreation below.*)

**Grand Canyon Overview Flights**

Some people prefer to see the canyon **by air**, which has certain advantages for those with limited time. You can certainly cover more ground by plane than you would by car. While flights have been restricted due to the noise pollution they cause, they are still available. Try **Grand Canyon Airlines** (*Tel. 800-528-2413. www.grandcanyonairlines.com*) for half-day trips from the Grand Canyon Airport. Tours start at $159. They also have a very popular daylong tour that includes a canyon over-flight as well as a raft float through part of the canyon on the Colorado River.

**Grand Canyon Railway**

To feel like you've stepped back in time, take the train from Williams to the Grand Canyon. Williams, 31-miles west of Flagstaff on I-40, is the origin of the famous **Grand Canyon Railway**. You'll start in a historic depot, built in 1910, and then board ornate coaches for the ride to the rim. Once there, you'll have 3.5 hours to either tour the rim by bus or explore around on your own. The roundtrip trip takes about eight hours. During your time on the train there is often music and entertainment. In the winter the train is transformed to the magical Polar Express. Reservations are recommended well in advance. *Info: Tel. 800-843-8724. www.thetrain.com. From $65 for adults and $29 for children under 10.*

## WHERE TO STAY
### SOUTH RIM

Xanterra Parks & Resorts, who have operations in many of the country's national parks, manage all of the hotels on the South Rim. There is one **central reservations number** (*Tel. 888-297-2757*) and one **reservations website** (*www.grandcanyonlodges.com*). They handle reservations for all hotels and dining on the South Rim. For **same day reservations**: *Tel. 928-638-2631.*

The Grand Canyon is very popular so please make your reservations well in advance. If you can't get lodging in the park, Tusayan has some hotels and is within "commuting" distance of the Grand Canyon. Be sure to call and check on last-minute availability if you haven't been able to reserve your dream choice. One time in the winter I was even able to get walk-up reservations at Phantom Ranch.

### El Tovar Hotel $$$

The first hotel to be built at the Grand Canyon, this wonderful establishment was built in 1905 and most recently renovated in 2005. The

architectural style, known as "rustic," aimed to create a structure that complemented its surroundings. You'll see native stone and massive pine logs throughout the building. Guestrooms range from small to very large, but are all nicely furnished. Some have amazing canyon views. The restaurant is outstanding. On the canyon rim. *Info: Tel. 888-297-2757. www.grandcanyonlodges.com. Grand Canyon Village. 78 rooms.*

## Kachina and Thunderbird Lodges $$

These sister properties are nearly identical in appearance and facilities and are literally connected. You can't really tell them apart. The rooms are simple, like a modern motel, but comfortable. The location however, is awesome. You are within walking distance of all the facilities of the Grand Canyon Village. Some rooms have canyon views. On the canyon rim. *Info: Tel. 888-297-2757. www.grandcanyonlodges.com. Grand Canyon Village. 49 and 55 rooms respectively.*

## Bright Angel Lodge $-$$

Built in 1935, the Bright Angel is one of the park's most historic properties. Designed by famous architect Mary J. Colter, the rustic style is more simple that than of El Tovar. Like the former, however, it features an attractive and comfortable lobby with a massive fireplace. The rooms are either in the main building or in small cabins. Eleven of the rooms do not have  private bath, but some larger rooms have fireplaces and canyon views. On the canyon rim. Restaurant and lounge. *Info: Tel. 888-297-2757. www. grandcanyonlodges.com. Grand Canyon Village. 88 rooms.*

### Yavapai Lodge $-$$

Nestled amid a forest of pinon and juniper trees, Yavapai is the largest hotel in the park. The motel-style rooms are very similar to those of Maswik. There are no views, but you have the convenience of staying in the park. Cafeteria and mini-mart. *Info: Tel. 888-297-2757. www.grandcanyonlodges.com. One mile from Grand Canyon Village. 358 rooms.*

### Maswik Lodge $

This modern lodge, with motel-style rooms, is spread out over several acres of ponderosa pine. (The north rooms are the largest.) There are also cabins available in the summer. The biggest benefit is that you are close to the Grand Canyon Village and rim. Cafeteria and lounge. *Info: Tel. 888-297-2757. www.grandcanyonlodges.com. One quarter mile from Grand Canyon Village. 248 rooms.*

### Tusayan Options

If you can't get a room in the park, try the national chains just outside the park in **nearby Tusayan**. Both **Holiday Inn Express** (*Tel. 800-315-2621, www.holidayinn.com*) and **Best Western** (*Tel. 800-780-7234, www.bestwestern.com*) have properties in Tusayan.

### Phantom Ranch $

If you want to spend the night on the canyon floor and don't want to camp, this is your only option. Located alongside Bright Angel Creek, Phantom Ranch was constructed in 1922 of uncut boulders taken from the Colorado River. Cabins are available for those taking the two-night mule trip. The other accommodations consist of men's and women's dormitories. The food, which you must reserve before you descend, is delicious. *Info: Tel. 888-297-2757. www.grandcanyonlodges.com. Canyon floor. 11 cabins. 10 bunk beds in each dormitory.*

**Desert View Campground $**
Fifty first-come, first-serve sites that offer wonderful canyon views and impressive sunrises. *Info: Tel. 928-638-7888.*

**Ten-X Campground $**
Seventy first-come, first-serve sites in the woods just south of the park entrance. *Info: Tel. 928-638-2443.*

# WHERE TO EAT
## SOUTH RIM
### El Tover Dining Room $$-$$$
Considering the informality of the Grand Canyon, you will be surprised at the formal nature of the dining experience at the El Tovar Dining Room. Although patrons are all dressed in hiking clothes, the servers are decked out in tuxedo shirts. If you can get reservations you should not miss dinner here. The room is spacious and attractive and the food is gourmet. Picture windows provide excellent views while you wait for your food. Excellent wine list. *Info: Tel. 888-297-2757. El Tovar Hotel in the Grand Canyon Village. Open for breakfast, lunch, and dinner daily. Reservations suggested.*

### Arizona Room $$
Located near the Bright Angel Lodge, the Arizona Room offers up tender, sizzling steaks. There are also chicken and fish dishes as well as salad. Here too, windows face the canyon. Cocktails and wine are served. *Info: Tel. 888-297-2757. Grand Canyon Village. Open for breakfast, lunch, and dinner daily.*

### Bright Angel Dining Room $
A more casual experience than at El Tovar, this restaurant features an ample selection of dishes including several vegetarian offerings. Service is friendly and efficient. Cocktails and wine are served. *Info: Tel. 888-297-2757. Bright Angel Lodge in the Grand Canyon Village. Open for breakfast, lunch, and dinner daily.*

# SHOPPING
## SOUTH RIM
All of the hotels and stores in the Grand Canyon offer souvenirs that range from silly t-shirts to wonderful works of art by Native American craftsmen. The **gift shop at El Tovar** on the South Rim is one of the nicer ones, while the one at the **Bright Angel Lodge** has an extensive array of items.

If you are headed from the South Rim to the North Rim, you will pass a number of trading posts, all of which carry Native American crafts. The largest and best of these is the **Cameron Trading Post**. With a large gift shop and wonderful gallery, they have it all. If you can't find a gift here, then it probably isn't made. *Info: www.camerontradingpost.com. 54 miles north of Flagstaff on Highway 89.*

## NIGHTLIFE & ENTERTAINMENT
### SOUTH RIM
Watching the sunset and listening to the crickets aren't the only way to pass the evening while at the Grand Canyon. There are, surprisingly, a number of other options. Bright Angel, El Tovar, and Mazwik Lodges on the South Rim all have occasional entertainment in their lounges. In addition, there are various programs throughout the year at the **Shrine of the Ages Theater** located adjacent to the Visitor Center, including a fantastic music festival in September. *Info: www.grandcanyonmusicfest.org.*

## SPORTS & RECREATION
### SOUTH RIM
### Biking
Bikes are allowed on all paved roads and other areas designated as bike accessible. Bike rentals are available in the park from **Bright Angel Bicycle Rentals** (*www.bikegrandcanyon.com*) at the Visitor Information Plaza near Mather Point. The **West Rim route**, when it is closed to car traffic, is an ideal bike ride. You can either ride the entire route or put your bike on a shuttle to take you up the first hill and then ride out the mostly flat road to Hermit's Rest from there. The views are amazing and you will have the road to yourself. In contrast, the **East Rim road has very little shoulder** and traffic can be quite heavy, making it a less-than-ideal bike route.

### South Rim Hiking
Hiking is the main draw as far as recreation in the canyon goes. Most of the hikes on the South Rim, with the exception of the Rim Trail, are steep and strenuous. If you are hiking down to the river to spend time at Phantom Ranch, it's nice to descend along the ridge of the **South Kaibab Trail** and ascend via the **Bright Angel Trail**. The **Grandview Trail**, which does not go down to the river, is a nice out and back to Horseshoe Mesa.

### Backcountry Hiking
If you want to overnight in the canyon, you must get a **backcountry permit**.

You can request a permit by mail *(Backcountry Office Grand Canyon National Park, P.O. Box 129, Grand Canyon, Arizona 86023)*, fax *(928-638-2125)*, or in person, but not by phone. You can request permits up to four months in advance. If you have questions, you can call the backcountry office (*Tel. 928-638-7888*) or check out their website at *www.nps.gov/grca/planyourvisit/backcountry-permit.htm*. You can rent camping equipment on the South Rim at **Babbitt's General Store**, *Tel. 928-638-2854*.

### Mule Trips & Tours

Mule trips are a very popular way to see the canyon, so it is suggested that reservations be made six to eight months in advance. There are two different trips. One is an overnight trip to the Phantom Ranch that includes lodging, breakfast, lunch, and dinner. The second trip is a three-hour round-trip ride along the new East Rim Trail. *Info: Tel. 888-297-2757. www.grandcanyonlodges.com/Mule-Trips-716.html. $132 for East Rim trip and $552 for the Phantom Ranch trip.* Rider qualifications include weight limit (200 pounds), height limit (must be at least 4'7") and English fluency.

### Rafting

Rafting the **Colorado River** through the Grand Canyon is an unforgettable experience. Both smooth and white water trips are offered. The smooth water trips take about 12 hours and include round-trip bus transportation

from the Grand Canyon Village. You'll float from the Glen Canyon Dam outside of Page, Arizona to Lee's Ferry, where the park officially starts. Contact **Colorado River Discovery** (*www.raftthecanyon.com, Tel. 888-522-6644*) for reservations and information. You may also make arrangements through **Grand Canyon National Park Lodges** for transportation from the South Rim to Page. *Info: 303-297-2757.*

Whitewater rafting on the Colorado is one of the world's great experiences. Although a few operators offer trips as short as three days, the majority of Grand Canyon rafting adventures are between six and nine days long. The season usually runs from April through October. You can contact the park office for a **list of concessionaires** (*www.nps.gov/grca/river, or Tel. 928-638-7843*). **Western River Expeditions** (*www.westernriver.com*) is a quality outfitter I have used. Plan on making your reservations far in advance if you wish to experience the canyon in this manner.

### Cross-Country Skiing

There are no groomed trails, but you are free to cross-country ski as conditions permit. Ski rentals are available at **Babbitt's General Store** in the Grand Canyon Village (*Tel. 928-638-2854*).

### DRIVING ROUTE TO THE NORTH RIM

While some people will be lucky enough to hike down the south side and back up to the North Rim, most visitors to the North Rim end up driving the 210 miles around the canyon from side to side. A good portion of the drive along AZ 64 to Cameron parallels the **Little Colorado River Gorge**. Along the road you'll pass several trading posts. Be on the lookout for them even if you aren't in the market for shopping because it is near these posts that short spur roads lead near the edge of the gorge. Brief walks will take you to the precipice. Be extra careful because some of the overlooks are not fenced in – hold onto your children!

At Cameron you can visit the historic **Cameron Trading Post**. Have a meal here, do some shopping, or just browse the incredible art gallery with rare and unique Native American pieces. From here, take 89 north to Bitter Spring and then follow 89A to AZ67 to the North Rim.

The drive from Bitter Spring to Marble Canyon is highly scenic with broad vistas of huge red sandstone cliffs surrounding an immense and equally colorful valley. **Marble Canyon**, which is actually located in a narrow strip of the eastern edge of Grand Canyon National Park, is a scene of great beauty that definitely merits a stop. Park at either end and walk over the **Navajo Bridge** which spans the Colorado River over a deep gorge that drops almost 800 feet to the water. With wonderful views of the gorge and river as well as the breathtaking backdrop of giant red sandstone cliffs, this is a great place for a picnic lunch.

Once you cross the river, you're in a part of the state known as the **Arizona Strip**. Before the construction of the Navajo Bridge, this portion of Arizona was physically cut off from the rest of the state. Highway 89A travels for 40 miles from here to Jacob Lake, climbing from monolithic red mountains to a more forested area. At Jacob Lake head south for 40 miles on AZ 67 through the thick greenery of the Kaibab National Forest until you reach the entrance to the North Rim.

## WHERE TO STAY & EAT
### SOUTH RIM TO NORTH RIM DRIVING ROUTE
**Cameron Trading Post Hotel $-$$**
Located at the historic Cameron Trading Post, the lodge offers comfortable rooms decorated in a southwestern motif. With views of the Little Colorado River Gorge, this is a good spot if you find yourself between the South and North Rims in the evening. Pleasant garden and good restaurant as well. *Info: Tel. 800-338-7385. www.camerontradingpost.com. Just north of Cameron. 66 rooms.*

**Cameron Trading Post Dining Room $**
The Cameron Trading Post would be worth a stop for a meal simply for the views of the Little Colorado River Gorge and the architecture of the dining room (the pressed tin ceiling is especially notable.) Luckily the food is good as well. Go for the Southwestern and Navajo-influenced dishes. *Info: Tel. 800-338-7385. Just north of Cameron. Open for breakfast, lunch, and dinner daily.*

**Marble Canyon Lodge Dining Room $**
Basic coffee shop and dining room in the middle of nowhere. Good place to stop en route. *Info: Tel. 928-355-2225. Immediately north of the Navajo Bridge on US-89A. Open for breakfast, lunch, and dinner daily.*

### NORTH RIM
Only about 10% of the visitors to the South Rim make it to the **North**

**Rim**, but those who do find the experience highly rewarding. The Grand Canyon Lodge is the hub of all activities here. Take note that the North Rim is generally only **open from the middle of May to the middle of October** depending on snow fall and melt. There are guided bus tours of the North Rim should you choose not to drive and one bus a day that travels from rim to rim.

Some of the best sights on the North Rim are located right by the lodge, not the least of which is the spectacular panorama available from the veranda of the lodge itself. But the real highlight of a North Rim visit involves taking the half-mile long **Bright Angel Point Trail** from directly behind the lodge out to Bright Angel Point. The trail is easy, but is entirely on an extremely narrow ridge that juts out into the canyon. There's a delightfully dizzying drop on either side.

If you want to hike, the **Transept Trail** stretches along the North Rim's edge for about three miles from the lodge area to the campground, while the **North Kaibab Trail** descends to the canyon floor at Phantom Ranch (an overnight trip).

There are some excellent vista points on the North Rim. Start with the 8,830-foot **Point Imperial** (*photo below*). This is the highest point on either rim and the view is dramatic and beautiful. You'll gaze eastward into a portion of the canyon not visible from anywhere on the South Rim's road system. It is

The **Cape Royal Drive** also has some great sights. These include the Vista Encantadora and the **Walhalla Overlook**. Be sure to also take the short trail to the **Angel's Window**, a large rock formation where erosion has carved out a giant hole.

Finally you'll arrive to **Cape Royal**, where one of the most colorful of all Grand Canyon vistas awaits. You'll see the **Granite Gorge**, as well as **Wotan's Throne**, a giant rock formation rising proudly from a plateau within the depths of the canyon. You'll also catch a panoramic view of canyon, forest, and distant mountains that is simply mesmerizing.

## WHERE TO STAY & EAT
### NORTH RIM
**Grand Canyon Lodge $-$$**
This is a wonderful place to stay because of the unparalleled natural setting and the charming accommodations. There are both motel-style room and  cabin rooms, but the outstanding cabins rooms facing the rim should be your first choice. The main building was constructed of limestone and massive timber beams in the 1930s. The outside verandas have one of the most beautiful views of the canyon found anywhere in the park. The restaurant is also excellent. Closed October-May. *Info: Tel. 888-297-2757. Same day reservations 928-638-2611. www.grandcanyonlodgenorth.com. On the rim. 165 cabins and 40 rooms.*

**North Rim Campground $**
Eighty-six sites, some reservable, on the rim facing the canyon. Great for sunset. *Info: Tel. 800-365-2267.*

**Grand Canyon Lodge Dining Room $-$$**
Like the lodge in which it is located, the dining room is a spacious facility with high timbered ceiling beams and simply breathtaking views of the canyon from two different directions. The service is quick and efficient. The selection of food is somewhat limited but nicely prepared. Cocktails available. *Info: Tel. 877-386-4383. Same day reservations 928-638-2611. www.grandcanyonlodgenorth.com. Open for breakfast, lunch, and dinner daily. Reservations recommended for dinner.*

*Note:* If you can't get a reservation at the North Rim, you can head for **Jacob Lake**, 45 miles away. Try the **Jacob Lake Inn** (*Tel. 928-643-7232, www.jacoblake.com*) or the first-come, first-serve **Jacob Lake Campground** (*Tel. 928-643-7395*).

## SPORTS & RECREATION
### NORTH RIM
#### North Rim Hiking

There are a handful of level trails on the North Rim. The **Bright Angel Point Trail** is a short (1/2 mile) trail out to a wonderful lookout area. The **Cape Final Trail**, about three miles roundtrip, offers wonderful rim views, as does the **Transept Trail**. The **North Kaibab Trail** leads into the canyon from the North Rim.

#### Havasu Falls

If you see a picture of lovely blue-green waterfalls, and the picture is in Arizona, it is probably from **Havasu Falls**. Located in a remote region of the western section of the Grand Canyon, the falls are accessible only by

hiking, horseback riding, or helicopter. If you've got the time and the stamina, it is definitely worth hiking the trip. (You can always arrange for a mule to haul your backpack, making for a much lighter load. Just be sure to take a day-pack with plenty of water for the hikes in and out.)

First you must hike eight miles to the village of **Supai**, where there is a small store and a lodge (*Tel. 928-448-2111*). If you are camping, you must hike two miles further to the campgrounds. The falls are in this area as well. Havasu, Mooeney, and Navaho Falls are all great photo spots as well as wonderful places to take a dip. *Info: Havasupai Tourist Enterprise, Supai, AZ 86435. Tel 928-448- 2121. www.nps.gov/grca/ planyourvisit/havasupai.htm $35 entry fee and additional charges for camping ($17) and the lodge ($145 Info: Tel. 928-448-2111).*

### Grand Canyon West Skywalk

The latest development along the Grand Canyon is the **Grand Canyon Skywalk** (see photo below), a glass bridge suspended at the edge of the canyon 4,000 above the Colorado River. Made out of more than one million pounds of steel, the bridge can sustain winds in excess of 100 miles per hour from 8 different directions, as well as an 8.0 magnitude earthquake within 50 miles. Other things to do in the area include a visit to the **Hualapai Ranch** for wagon rides, cookouts, and horseback riding or rafting a section of the Colorado River. The whole area, privately owned and operated by the Haulapai Tribe, is mainly set up for visitors from Las Vegas. *Info: www. grandcanyonwest.com. Tel. 888-868- 9378. 80 miles northwest of Kingman, 120 miles east of Las Vegas. It costs $72 per person to see and walk on bridge.*

# 7. Northeastern Arizona

**HIGHLIGHTS**

• **Hopi Mesas** – Walpi on the First Mesa

• **Canyon de Chelly** – South Rim Drive, Canyon Tour

• **Monument Valley** – Valley Drive, hike or horseback ride

• **Navajo National Monument** – Betatkin Ruin

• **Lake Powell** – Glen Canyon, Rainbow Bridge; Antelope Canyon

This vast, sparsely populated region has been home to both the Navajo and Hopi peoples for centuries. Blessed with impressive sandstone rock formations, beautiful canyons, and well-preserved ruins, the Navajo Nation, which covers most of the region, is also fascinating from a cultural standpoint. Equally fascinating is the small **Hopi Reservation** surrounded entirely by the Navajo Nation. You can visit the three mesas that the Hopi have occupied for centuries, learn about their way of life, and have the opportunity to buy incredible hand-crafted art.

In the northwestern corner of the region you'll find the impressive **Lake Powell**, part of the **Glen Canyon National Recreation Area**, and a boater's dream.

## ORIENTATION

**I-40** cuts east to west across northeastern Arizona (as does **US 160** further north) and provides easy access from Phoenix. **US 89** is another major point of entry. The Navajo Nation lands completely surround the Hopi Nation lands.

## SEEING THE SIGHTS

The distances between sights are far in this part of the state, but the pay-off is some of the most incredible landscapes in the country. From soaring canyon walls to nature-sculpted rock formations, the wonders present here will stay with you forever. You'll learn about native cultures as well as appreciate the fantastic beauty of the national monuments and parks.

### THE NAVAJO NATION

The Navajo Nation, which extends from Arizona into Utah and Nevada, covers 27,000 square miles. Within its borders are an amazing number of national monuments, historical sites, and tribal parks that merit visits.

### Canyon de Chelly National Monument

Located about two miles east of the town of Chinle, **Canyon de Chelly** is one of the highlights of the Navajo Nation. The canyon, although not as deep as the Grand Canyon, is special for both its beauty and historical importance. The sheer red sandstone walls of the canyon, ranging from 30 to more than 1,000 feet in height, create a spectacular backdrop for hundreds of **Anasazi ruins**, as well as present-day **Navajo farms**.

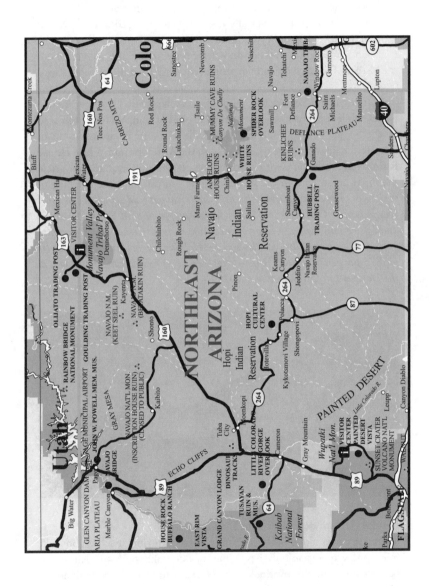

**You must have a guide to enter the canyon**, which you can do on either a full or a half-day tour. Although you can take your own 4x4 vehicle with the guide, I really recommend hiring a jeep or joining one of the tours. That way you can just sit back and take in the amazing contrast of the red walls and the verdant valley without worrying about getting stuck in the deep sand. Your guide will not only drive for you, but also tell you about the history of the canyon and the people who have lived there over the ages.

The canyon itself is remarkable. Smooth red walls soar up 1,000 feet at some places, while cottonwoods grow along side plots of land that have been used by the Navajo people for years. Your guide will stop at various points of interest and give you time to admire both the **Antelope and White House Ruins**, remarkable ancient cliff dwellings. It's best to arrange your guide the night before, but in the slower seasons you can do it the morning of your trip. *Info: www.nps.gov/cach. Information about guides and the canyon at the Canyon de Chelly Visitors Center (open daily from 8am-5pm). Horseback and hiking tours can also be arranged at the Visitor's Center. Arrange group-guided trips through the tour desks at the Holiday Inn or Thunderbird Lodge for $75 per person. Private 3-hour trips start at $175 and can be arranged at the Holiday Inn (See Where to Sleep).*

**On the Canyon de Chelly Rim**
There are drives along both the South and North rims. Each is about 25 miles one way. If you only have time for one, take the South Rim drive because it has the best overlooks. The **North Rim Drive** extends along the Canyon del Muerto arm of the park and has four overlooks.

On the **South Rim Drive**, be sure to stop at the **White House Overlook** where you can see the White House cliff dwelling built into the rocks on the other side of the canyon. There's a great trail at the White House Overlook that leads down to the canyon floor. This is a steep hike with some sheer drop-offs, but well worth it if you're fit. Continue along the South Rim Drive to the **Spider Rock Overlook** at the end of the drive. Be sure to walk to the end of the overlook for a magical view of Spider Rock standing 830 feet tall at a junction in the canyon floor. The colors of the canyon walls are spectacular from here as well.

## WHERE TO STAY & EAT
### CANYON DE CHELLY/CHINLE
**Holiday Inn $$**
Just a half-mile from the park entrance, this Holiday Inn is located at was once Garcia's Trading Post. That gives it much more charm than you would usually get from a chain hotel. It has a few more amenities than the Sacred Canyon lodge, like an outdoor pool and high-speed internet. The restaurant is good as well. Canyon tours available. *Info: Tel. 928-674-5000. www.holidayinn.com. Half-mile from the entrance to Canyon de Chelly. Indian Route 7 - Garcia Trading Post. 108 rooms.*

**Thunderbird Lodge $-$$**
Not only does the Thunderbird Lodge provide the convenience of staying right in Canyon de Chelly National Monument, it is also a very pleasant and attractive facility. You cannot see the canyon from the lodge (even though the hotel is only seven hundred yards from the beginning of it), because the lodge is surrounded by a large grove of beautiful cottonwood trees. There are two sections of the lodge – the older rooms are smaller, but you really can't go wrong in either section. The cafeteria style restaurant is surprising good. Operated by the Navajo Nation. Canyon tours available. *Info: Tel. 800-679-2473. thunderbirdlodge.com. In Canyon de Chelly National Monument. 72 rooms.*

If these two are full, try the **Best Western** in Chinle, just two miles from the park (*Tel. 800-780-7234, www.bestwestern.com*).

**Garcia's at the Holiday Inn $**
The only table-served restaurant near the park, Garcia's is a good bet after a long day of touring. The homemade bread is quite good although you'll have to ask for more kick in the southwestern dishes if you like spicy food.

*Info: Tel. 928-674-5000. One half mile outside the entrance to Canyon del Chelly: Indian Route 7 - Garcia Trading Post. Open for breakfast, lunch and dinner daily.*

### Sacred Canyon Lodge Dining Room $

This multi-room dining facility offers a good variety of American, South-western, and Native American food. It is served café style, but is still excellent. The restaurant is located in the original trading post and in the center is a vault-like room that once served at as jail. Beautiful Navajo rugs and other crafts decorate the walls. *Info: Tel. 800-679-2473. In Canyon de Chelly National Monument. Open daily for breakfast, lunch and dinner.*

### MONUMENT VALLEY NAVAJO TRIBAL PARK

You'll recognize the unique images of **Monument Valley** as soon as you arrive, due to their ubiquitous presence in TV commercials, movies, and print advertising. The large buttes, mesas, and canyons compete for your attention with unusual freestanding rock formations. Some of them can be best described by simply stating their names – The Mittens, Elephant Butte,

the Three Sisters, and The Thumb for example. A few of these amazing sandstone monoliths rise to heights of 1,000 feet above the valley.

Stop first at the visitor's center and then take the **17-mile self-guided Valley Drive**, which passes most of the major formations at 11 marked stops. It's definitely worth getting out of the car to go on the walk from North Window to Cly Butte. Both horseback and jeep tours are available into parts of the park that can only be visited with a guide. Make arrangements in the parking lot at the visitor's center. If you want to hike on your own, the Wildcat Trail is phenomenal. The 3.3 mile path leaves from near the visitor's center and wraps around West Mitten Butte. *Info: Tel. 435-727-5875. www.navajonationparks.org. Open daily 6am-8pm (May-September)* *or 8am-5pm (October-April.) Per vehicle charge $20 (up to four people), additional people $6 each, children under 7 free.*

## WHERE TO STAY & EAT
### MONUMENT VALLEY
#### Goulding's Lodge $-$$
Although technically in Utah, Goulding's Lodge is very much a part of the Monument Valley environs and history, located adjacent to the park. The accommodations are pretty basic motel-style rooms, but they all have balconies with wonderful views of Monument Valley. Be sure to ask if any of the three houses are available. They cost the same as hotel rooms and offer full kitchens and fireplaces. House #340 has one of the most amazing views you'll ever experience anywhere. Many film crews and stars have stayed here over the years. Good restaurant. Tours available. Pool and wireless internet. *Info: Tel. 435-727-3231. www.gouldings.com. Monument Valley, UT. 62 rooms. 3 houses.*

#### The View Hotel $-$$
This excellent hotel, located inside the park, offers breathtaking views of the sculptured rocks. Situated so that all rooms have unblocked views of the famous formations and designed to blend in with the surrounding landscape, there is not a bad room in the house. You'll be tempted to sit on your patio and enjoy the scenery all day. There are even westward-facing sunset balconies for all to enjoy. The rooms are standard for hotels in the category, with flat screen TVs, microwaves, and coffee makers. Wi-Fi available in reception area only. Guided tours of the park can be arranged through the hotel. Restaurant located next door at the visitors center. *Info: monumentvalleyview. com. Tel. 435-727-5556. Monument Valley National Tribal Park. 96 rooms.*

If you can't get a room at Gouldings or The View, **Kayenta**, 25 miles south, is the closest town with lodging. The best choices there are the **Hampton Inn** (*Tel. 800-426-7866. www.hamptoninn.com*) and the **Holiday Inn** (*Tel. 800-315-2621. www.holidayinn.com*).

#### Stagecoach Dining Room at Goulding's Lodge $
The dining room at Goulding's offers wonderful looks at Monument Valley. You'll enjoy sitting in front of the view windows eating Navajo-influenced dishes. *Info: Tel. 435-727-3231. Monument Valley, UT. Open daily for breakfast, lunch and dinner.*

**The View Restaurant $**
Located next door to the View Hotel inside Monument Valley Park, the restaurants offers affordable and tasty Navajo-inspired dishes. The mutton stew with fry bread is a specialty. Be advised, because it is on the reservation, no alcohol is served. *Info: Tel. 435-727-5556. Monument Valley National Tribal Park. Open daily for breakfast, lunch, and dinner.*

## NAVAJO NATIONAL MONUMENT
Impressive and stunningly beautiful, the **Navajo National Monument** protects **three pueblo ruins** dating from the 13<sup>th</sup> century. Preserved beneath enormous cliffs, the ruins are in pristine condition. Two of them, **Betatakin** and **Keet Seel** can only be visited by ranger-conducted tours. Both involve strenuous walks of five and 16 miles respectively. The tours are at different times depending on demand and the season, so call a few days before you plan to visit. Betatakin, which means House on the Ledge, is sheltered in a vast cave in the cliff. It's almost as if a futuristic dome has been built over a strange city. It is so remarkable that it is probably my favorite ruin in Arizona. The hike takes you down to the remarkably preserved ruin, which you are allowed to walk through with your guide. You can also see Betatakin without taking the hike by following a paved pathway from the visitor's center to an overlook that provides an excellent view of the ruin. *Info: Tel. 928-672-2700. www.nps.gov/nava/index.htm. Free entry.*

### Hubbell Trading Post National Historic Site
John Hubbell established the post in 1878 and he soon became one of the foremost Indian traders in the American southwest. You can stop by the visitor center as well as tour the Hubbell home, which looks much as it did at the time it was acquired by the Hubbell family. Native American's display and sell their crafts and weaving demonstrations are given. It is interesting to note that the trading post still serves the same purpose today as it did in the last century. *Info: Tel. 928-755-3475. www.nps.gov/hutr/index.htm. Open daily 8am-5pm (6pm in summer.) Free admission, but guided tours of the house cost $2 per person.*

### Window Rock Navajo Tribal Park & Veteran's Memorial
The **capital of the Navajo Nation**, this side trip is worth a couple of hours if you are interested in Navajo culture because of the **Navajo Nation Museum** located here. The museum offers a complete history of the Navajo people as well as the natural history of the Four Corners region. *Info: Tel. 928-871-7941. www.navajonationmuseum.org. 8am-6pm daily except Sunday.*

The city is named for an impressive round hole ("window") in the sandstone above the city. At the base of the Window Rock you'll find the **Window Rock Navajo Tribal Park and Veteran's Memorial** to honor the many Navajos who served in the U.S. military. Especially important were the Code Talkers, who used their native Navajo language to create a code that was never broken by during World War II. *Info:navajonationparks.org/html/veterans.htm .Open daily 8am-7pm. Admission free.*

## SHOPPING
### NAVAJO NATION
The gift shops at the lodges as well as the numerous trading posts in the Navajo Nation offer Native American jewelry, crafts, rugs and mementos. The **Hubbell Trading Post** is one of the best. You'll even find crafts for sale deep in Canyon de Chelly at the White House ruins.

### 4 States at Once!
Even though it's kind of silly, plenty of people (including your au-thor) drive out of their way to the Four Corners Monument, where Arizona, New Mexico, Colorado, and Utah meet. You can stand on the brass marker and be in all four states at the same time. There is also a Navajo crafts market there. *Info: navajonationparks.org/html/fourcornershours.htm. 8am-5pm daily. (8am-7pm in summer.) Admis-sion $5 for all over 7 and over.*

## NIGHTLIFE & ENTERTAINMENT
### NAVAJO NATION
There is very little happening in terms of nightlife in the Navajo nation. Remember, there is no alcohol allowed on the reservation. There is, however, a casino. The **Twin Arrows Navajo Casino Resort**, located off I-40 about 20 miles east of Flagstaff (*exit 219, www.twinarrows.com*), offers gaming, dining, lodging, and a spa.

## SPORTS & RECREATION
### NAVAJO NATION
#### Hiking
Most hiking on the reservation must be done with a guide. The exceptions to this are the wonderful **White House Ruins Trail** at Canyon de Chelly, and the **Wildcat Trail** in Monument Valley.

If you want to hike with a guide, the **Betatakin and Keet Seel hikes** at the Navajo National Monument are phenomenal. You can also take guided hikes into Canyon de Chelly and Monument Valley.

#### Horseback Riding
Horseback riding can be arranged at both Canyon del Chelly and Monument Valley. Your hotel will be able to help you make arrangements, or, in the off-season, you can just show up the day before and arrange it yourself.

### HOPI MESAS
The **Hopi Reservation**, completely surrounded by the Navajo Nation and off of the main roads, receives fewer visits from tourists than does the Navajo Nation. If you are interested in learning more about Native American cultures, there is quite a lot to see here. The Hopi, who claim to be descendants of the Anasazi, have lived in the area since the 12th century. Most of the Hopi villages are concentrated on three mesas off of AZ-264. Each of the villages is known for making certain Hopi crafts. Keep in mind that **no photography is allowed** on the Hopi Reservation and that some villages are off limits to visitors on certain days of the year.

#### First Mesa
Known for **pottery** and **katsina dolls**, the villages of the First Mesa merit a visit for the one-hour walking tour offered here. Situated on the edge of steep cliffs with amazing views beyond, the village of **Walpi**, at the end of the tour, is sure to be a highlight of your trip. Tours usually leave Ponsi Hall

in Sichomovi 9:30am–5pm daily in summer and 10am-3pm daily the rest of the year. It's best to call ahead however to double check the schedule. *Info: Tel. 928-737-2262. Off-AZ 264 just past milepost 392: First Mesa Village. $8 adult, $5 children 6–17.*

### Second Mesa
Besides presenting an opportunity to shop for Hopi crafts, there is an excellent museum here. The Hopi Cultural Center has an outstanding collection of all kinds of Hopi crafts. You'll also learn about the ancestral spirits that play such an important role in Hopi life. *Info: Tel 928-734-2401. www. hopiculturalcenter.com. Highway AZ-264. Open 8am-5pm weekdays and 9am-3pm on weekends. $3 Adults. $1 children under 13.*

### Third Mesa
The villages of the Third Mesa are known for their weavings of both cloth and baskets. Stop at Kykotsmovi to get permits to visit the rest of the villages on the mesa, including Oraibi, which may be the oldest continually inhabited village in the US.

## WHERE TO STAY & EAT
### HOPI MESAS
#### Moenkopi Legacy Inn and Suites $$
Located in what seems like Tuba City, but is actually across the street from the

the city line, the Moenkopi is the first hotel built on Hopi lands in 50 years. New and high quality – it's a welcome addition to the area lodging options. Decorated with lots of Hopi art. Restaurant and pool on site. *Info: Tel. 928-283-4500. www.experiencehopi.com/hotel.html. Near Tuba City at intersection of Highways 160 and 264.*

### Hopi Cultural Center Motel $

Very simple motel-style rooms, but the only place to stay in the center of the mesas. There is a restaurant here as well as a museum. *Info: Tel. 928-734-2401. www.hopiculturalcenter.com. Second Mesa. 33 rooms.*

### Hopi Cultural Center Restaurant $

Run by the Hopi people, this restaurant offers many authentic Hopi dishes. *Info: Tel. 928-734-2401. Second Mesa. Open daily for breakfast, lunch, and dinner.*

## Hopi Culinary Treats

If you're not going to spend the night on the Hopi Reservation, you should plan to fill your belly and your tank at the **Hopi Cultural Center** (*Tel. 928-734-2401*). The restaurant offers you a chance to sample Hopi dishes, like **blue-corn pancakes**. If you are going to spend the night here, make your reservations well in advance.

# LAKE POWELL & GLEN CANYON NATIONAL RECREATION AREA

**Lake Powell**, which was created by the construction of the **Glen Canyon Dam**, is a thing of beauty. Shining a deep blue in the almost guaranteed brilliant sunshine, the lake is 186 miles long and surrounded by towering red sandstone cliffs. Dozens of side canyons, some small and some quite large, add to its mystery for boaters. In the distance is 10,388-foot high Navajo Mountain. The town of **Page** is the headquarters of the vast **Glen Canyon**

**National Recreation Area** on and around Lake Powell. Page didn't exist until 1956 when construction of a great dam on the Colorado River began.

### Visitor Centers

Make at stop at the **Carl Hayden Visitor's Center** at the **Glen Canyon Dam** nestled on the very edge of the canyon wall between the dam's front face and the bridge over the **Colorado River**. Far less known than the Hoover Dam, the Glen Canyon Dam is equal if not better in terms of both structure and setting. Take in the view from the outdoor observation deck, where the river flows hundreds of feet below you. The dam is 710 feet high and its crest is 1560 feet long. You can also take an elevator down to the base of the dam where you get extraordinary views of the canyon. *Info: Tel. 928-608-6072. Open daily 8am-5pm (6pm in summer). Tours $5.*

While in Page you can check out the **John Wesley Powell Memorial Museum**. With information on Powell's expeditions through the Grand Canyon as well as displays of Native American artifacts, it's an interesting stop. The museum is also a visitor information center where you can book different boat and land tours. *Info: www.powellmuseum.org. Tel. 928-645-9496. www.powellmuseum.org. Corner of Lake Powell Blvd and Navajo Dr.: 6 North Lake Powell Blvd. 9am-5pm Monday-Saturday. $3 age 16-61, $2 age 61 and over, $1 age 15 and younge.*

### Lake & Lakeside Attractions

While a small portion of the lake and the encompassing scenery is visible from land, the only good way to see the area is by boat, since few roads penetrate any portion of the **Glen Canyon National Recreation Area**. I recommend that you take one of the **boat tours** offered at the Lake Powell (Wahweap) Marina. (There are public boat ramps here too if you arrive with your own vessel.) Boat trips vary from as short as an hour to all day. Probably

the most popular is the all-day tour to **Rainbow Bridge National Monument**. This incredible sight is the largest known natural bridge in the world. With a height of 270 feet, the bridge really has to be seen to be appreciated. Depending on lake levels, you may have to hike about a mile to get to the Rainbow Bridge once you dock. Other tours go to Antelope and Navajo Canyons or just around the bay (see photo at right). *Info: Tel. 800-528-6154. www. lakepowell.com. Prices vary from $45 to $175 depending on the cruise chosen and the time of year.*

**Antelope Canyon's** narrow, red slot ravines, with their rays of sunlight streaming down, are an almost iconic image of Arizona. Photographers flock here, but even if you aren't interested in pictures, it's worth a visit because the scenery is amazing. The upper canyon is easy to access – your guide will just drive right up. For this reason it is more crowded than the lower section of the canyon. The lower canyon, which requires using ladders to access, is for the more adventurous. Either way you have to go with a guide because it is on Navajo land. *Info: navajonationparks.org/html/antelopetours.htm.*

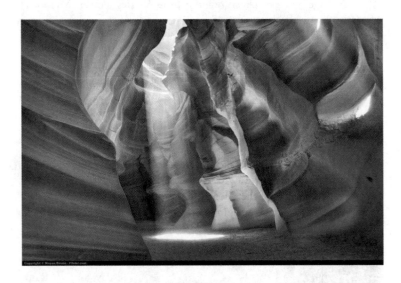

## WHERE TO STAY & EAT
**LAKE POWELL**
**Lake Powell Resort $$-$$$**
Spread out on the shoreline of magnificent Lake Powell, the setting of this resort makes it worth a stay. The two-story motor inn type buildings feature rooms that are reasonable attractive and comfortable. All have a patio or balcony, but those that face the lake have the best views. Amenities include two heated swimming pools and a workout area. This is also the

place for boat rentals and boat tours, so staying here makes it convenient to access those activities. The dining room is nice although a bit expensive, but there is also a pizza restaurant on site. *Info: Tel. 800-528-6154. www. lakepowell.com. Four miles north of Page on the shores of Lake Powell: 100 Lakeshore Dr. 350 rooms.*

**Best Western Arizonainn $-$$**
Yes, the spelling is correct – no space between Arizona and inn. This attractive motel is located at the top of a hill that overlooks Lake Powell and the Glen Canyon Dam. If your room faces in that direction then you're in for a special treat. It's definitely worth spending a few dollars more for the vistas. The location is convenient for activities on both the lake and in town. Heated swimming pool, restaurant, and free continental breakfast. *Info: Tel. 800-826-2718. www.bestwestern.com. 716 Rimview Drive. 103 rooms.*

**Lake Powell Days Inn & Suites $-$$**
One of the newest hotels in town, this is a good choice for families as there are 22 suites that not only include a separate living space with a sofa bed, but also microwaves and refrigerators. The pool is a pleasant place to cool off after a day of adventuring. Nice views of Lake Powell. Breakfast included. *Info: Tel. 877-525-3769. www.daysinn.net. In Page: 961 N. US 89. 82 rooms.*

**Bonkers Restaurant $$-$**
Bonkers is best known and loved locally for their Italian dishes, but they also serve up tasty burgers and sandwiches. Beer and wine are offered. *Info: Tel. 928-645-2706. 810 N. Navajo Dr. Dinner served nightly. Reservations recommended.*

**Dam Bar & Grille $**
Decked out in the full "dam" theme, including hard hats on the concrete walls, this restaurant is definitely part of the Page scene. Great prime rib, but also yummy burgers and salads. *Info: Tel: 928-645-2161. 644 N. Navajo Dr.*

# SPORTS & RECREATION
## LAKE POWELL
### Boating
Almost any kind of boat, power or sail, is allowed and available for rental. Be aware, however, that small boats can be dangerous during storms when Lake Powell can become rather turbulent.

**House boating** is an extremely popular way to experience Lake Powell. The boats are available for rent all over Page, but the easiest to coordinate is probably with the **Lake Powell Resort** at the Wahweap Marina (*Tel. 800-528-6154, www.lakepowell.com*). All boats, regardless of size, feature walkways, range, oven, refrigerator, ice chest, heater, shower, toilet, charcoal grill, and bunk-style beds. All necessary supplies, including a full tank of gas, are furnished to you except that you must provide your own bedding, linens and food. They don't require any special skills or prior boating experience except for an understanding of basic boating rules and courtesy. Be sure to buy a detailed map of the lake at the time of rental.

## Fishing

Bass, trout, and crappie are all popular catches in Lake Powell. An Arizona fishing license is required. You may also be required to have a Utah fishing license if fishing from a boat. You can secure both locally.

## Rafting

You can experience a **float trip** down a smooth portion of the Colorado River. You'll travel on the river through beautiful sandstone cliffs from the Glen Canyon Dam to Lee's Ferry, the official start of the Grand Canyon. Check out **Wilderness River Adventures** (*www.riveradventures.com, Tel. 928-645-3279*) for more information.

## Water Sports

Swimmers will find **beaches in the Wahweap area** and throughout the lake. **Water skiing** is done mainly in the wider channels and bays of the lake. Be alert for marked areas where water skiing is prohibited.

## Kayaking & Paddle Boarding

**Kayaking** and **paddle boarding** are becoming increasingly popular on the lake. You can rent kayaks at the marina and head out on your own, or go with a guide and see things you might not experience otherwise.

*Info: www.lakepowellhidden-canyonkayak.com for kayak rentals and tours and www.lakepowellpaddleboards.com for paddleboard rentals and tours.*

# 8. EASTERN ARIZONA

## HIGHLIGHTS

• **Petrified Forest National Park**

• **Turquoise Room** at La Posada

• **Coronado Trail to Hannagan Meadow**

• Hiking, fishing, skiing, or horseback riding in **Greer**

The geography of Eastern Arizona ranges from colorful desert landscapes to alpine forests. The northern portion of the region boasts the **Painted Desert**, historic **Route 66**, and the railroad towns of **Winslow** and **Holbrook**. Making your way south you'll come to the less-visited but lush and verdant **Apache-Sitgreaves National Forest**.

Outdoors lovers are in heaven here; the area has miles of hiking and biking trails, excellent trout stream and lakes, reliable snow skiing, and the nation's only designated "primitive area" where no mechanized transportation, including bikes, is allowed. The pleasant hamlet of Greer is located in the heart of the region, but recreation opportunities also exist to the west in **Pinetop-Lakeside** and **Payson**.

## ORIENTATION
The Petrified Forest is located off of I-40; get to Apache-Sitgreaves National Forest via US-191. Payson is off of AZ-87. Pinetop-Lakeside is off of AZ-260 and Greer, in the White Mountains, is off of AZ-373

## SEEING THE SIGHTS
### WINSLOW/HOLBROOK
Made famous from the line in the Eagle's song *Take it Easy*, many people make a stop for standin' on the corner in Winslow, Arizona. You too can stop by Standin' on the Corner Park and have your picture taken with the

Bill Morrow

statue of a young hitchhiker. *Info: Downtown Winslow on the NW corner of Kinsley Avenue and Second St.*

Even if you are not staying in Winslow overnight, you should check out the charming and historic **La Posada Hotel**. Created to look like a Spanish hacienda, La Posada was designed by Mary Colter, chief architect and designer for the Fred Harvey Company. Recently restored, this famous railroad hotel is now home to what some consider the best restaurant in the entire Four Corners Region – the **Turquoise Room**. Recreating the elegant dining experience of the Turquoise Room dining car on the Santa Fe's Super Chief, the restaurant offers fantastic fare in a wonderful setting. Start with the Route 66 Cadillac Margarita and all will be well in the world.

Just north of Winslow is **Homolovi Ruins State Park**. These pueblos, dating from the 14th century, were occupied by the ancestors of the modern

day Hopi. This is a sacred site to them, so tread with respect. *Info: Off I-40 at Exit 257. Tel. 928-289-4106. azstateparks.com/Parks/HORU. Open 8am-5pm daily. $7 adults.*

One of the largest attractions in the region is the **Petrified Forest National Park**, a unique Arizona attraction. About 225 million years ago, tall trees on what was once a giant flood plain fell and were covered by silt and mud. Mineral deposits in the ground water seeped into the logs and crystallized, turning the trees into brightly colored petrified wood. These fallen "trees," now as hard as stone, are scattered across the desert in this National Park.

The 29-mile park road, which runs north-south, can be driven in either direction. I'll take it from north to south for this description. The first part of the drive offers excellent views of the **Painted Desert**. Stop at some or all of the eight overlooks along the rim top to enjoy sweeping and ever-changing views. Take the easy one-mile **Painted Desert Rim Trail** between Tawa and Kachina Points if you like to walk.

The **Newspaper Rock Overlook** is worth a stop as it looks down on a huge sandstone rock covered with petroglyphs. Don't miss the easy trails through the colorful petrified wood at the **Crystal Forest** and the huge specimens at **Giant Logs**. The **Agate House Trail** leads to a semi-restored pueblo

constructed entirely of petrified wood. The **Rainbow Forest Museum** at the southern end of the park is worth a stop if you're interested in dinosaur skeletons. *Info: Off I-40 at exit 311. Tel. 928-524-6228. www.nps.gov/pefo. Open 8am-7pm daily. (7am-7pm or 8pm in summer) $20 per vehicle.*

### Leave it Alone!

While it is very tempting to pick up a piece of petrified wood and slip it in your pocket, you really shouldn't do it. **Not only is it against the law, it is also bad luck!** (Check out the letters at the visitor centers from those who took wood home with them and suffered terrible fates.) There are many places in Holbrook that legally sell petrified wood coming from outside the park.

The southern end of the park is very near the town of **Holbrook**. The "Mother Road," **Route 66**, runs right through town, and most of the establishments along the route have kept the look from their 1950s glory days. If you're in town at meal time, **Joe & Aggie's Mexican Café** (*120 W. Hope Dr., Tel. 928-524-6450*) offers excellent food with classic Route 66 kitsch.

## WHERE TO STAY & EAT
### WINSLOW
**La Posada Hotel $$**
Back in the day when travel by railroad was the best way to go, elegant hotels were built along the route to continue that first-class experience after travelers left the rail. La Posada, a hacienda designed by famous architect Mary Colter (who also designed many Grand Canyon buildings), is one of these hotels. Restored to its 1930s grandeur, La Posada is a wonderful place to spend a day or two. The rooms, decorated with period pieces, are delightful spots to sit and look out at the garden or passing trains. No phones in rooms, although they do have cable TV. The Turquoise Room restaurant is worth a stop even if you're not spending the night. *Info: www.laposada. org. Tel. 928-289-4366. 303 E. Second Street (Route 66). 38 rooms.*

**Turquoise Room at La Posada Hotel $$$**
The Santa Fe Railroad's Super Chief was so

luxurious that it became the favorite train of celebrities traveling across country. The "Train of the Stars" had an unmatched private dining car called the Turquoise Room. Recreating that type of elegant dining experience, this restaurant offers fantastic fare in a wonderful setting. The Route 66 Cadillac Margarita is a splendid start to any meal and goes well with the pork carnitas. *Info: www.laposada.org/turquoise-room.html. Tel 928-289-4366. 303 E. Second Street (Route 66). Open daily breakfast, lunch, and dinner. Dinner reservations recommended.*

## THE WHITE MOUNTAINS

Generally contiguous with the **Apache-Sitgreaves National Forest**, the White Mountains are unusual in Arizona. These heavily forested mountains appear more like the mountains of the East Coast than the usually more arid-looking western peaks. There are also a large number of natural lakes. With elevations generally in the five to six-thousand-foot level, the weather is cooler and there is more rainfall than in other parts of the state. The result is a vast oasis and popular playground for Phoenix residents. Outside of Arizona the area is not well known at all, but it merits a visit if you've got the time. (The Apache-Sitgreaves Nation Forest was the site of the largest fire in Arizona history in 2011. The forest is rebounding, as nature takes its course, but here are still some areas that are restricted due to danger of falling timber.)

In the sister cities of **Springerville** and **Edgar**, you'll have a chance to visit the **Casa Malpais Pueblo**. There is a museum onsite with displays about the Mogollon Indian culture. Guided tours of the 15-acre ruin site are offered as well. The pueblo, built around 1250, contains the main pueblo with more than 100 rooms and the Great Kiva. *Info: www.casamalpais.org. 318 Main St. in Springerville. Tel. 928-333-5375. 8am-4pm Monday through Saturday. Tours at 9am, 11am, and 2pm. Tour $10 adults, $5 18 and under.*

### Frontier Women
Across from the Springerville post office on Main Street you'll see the **Madonna of the Trail**, one of 12 statues built in the 1930s in various parts of the country to honor the spirit of America's pioneer women. Clothed in frontier dress and a large sunbonnet, the statue holds both a rifle and an infant, which seems to be the ultimate in multi-tasking.

Continue south on the section of Highway 191 known as the **Coronado Trail**. The route is reported to trace the course that Francisco Vasquez de Coronado followed in search of the Golden Seven Cities of Cibola in 1540. Enjoy the curving drive along forests, meadows and lakes that highlights the beauty of the high mountain scenery. The route officially runs all the way to Clifton, but you can stop at Hannagan Meadow for a few days of R&R.

The remote **Hannagan Meadow**, elevation 9100-feet, is a wonderful stopping point for outdoor activities on thousands of acres of beautiful forests and trails. You can hike, horseback ride, fish, camp, hunt, mountain bike and ski in the area. You might also see a **gray wolf**, as this is site where the endangered species reintroduction program was started in 1997.

Stay, eat, and recreate at the Hannagan Meadow Lodge or camp at the Hannagan Campground. Oh, and pay your bills when you leave: Hannagan Meadow was named for rancher Robert Hannagan who, in the early 1900's, was chained to a tree until his son paid off his $1200 debt. You wouldn't want the same to happen to you!

You can also access the **Blue Range Primitive Area** from here. The last Primitive Area in the United States, it is off-limits to all motorized and mechanized vehicles – even bicycles!

## WHERE TO STAY & EAT
### HANNAGAN MEADOW
**Hannagan Meadow Lodge $-$$**
While the accommodations and dining are pretty simple here, the location is out of this world. Situated at 9100 feet in the Apache-Sitgreaves National Forest, Hannagan Meadow is a wonderful getaway. If you love outdoor activities, you'll be in heaven here. Photographers come for the wildlife...birds, elk, coyotes, deer and even wolves. The cabins are equipped with kitchens and the lodge rooms include breakfast. The home-style restaurant is open for certain meals only, depending on the season. There is also a general store that

offers basic grocery items, snacks and drinks. *Info: www.hannaganmeadow. com. Tel. 928-339-4370. 22 miles south of Alpine on the Coronado Trail (US 191). 8 lodge rooms. 10 cabins.*

**Greer**, at the end of AZ-373, is another excellent destination for R&R. An outdoor enthusiast's paradise on the banks of the **Little Colorado River** (*see photo below*). Greer offers many of the same activities of Hannagan Meadow but in a more "civilized" environment. There are lodges and inns that cater to all budgets.

With rolling meadows, heavily-reed forests, and gentle mountain slopes, the land around Greer offers numerous active pursuits. Anglers rave about the trophy trout found in the area's lakes, reservoirs and streams, while hikers make tracks on the soft paths that lead through stands of pine and aspen.

Two wonderful hikes include the 8-mile one-way **Mount Baldy Trail**, which climbs almost all the way to the summit of 11,590-ft **Mount Baldy**, Arizona's second highest peak and the shorter, but equally beautiful trail that summits Escudilla Mountain, the state's third highest pinnacle.

There are also plenty of **antique stores**, as well as the quaint **Butterfly Lodge Museum**. The museum, once the home of a western writer and his artist son, displays artifacts and information about their lives. *Info: On the left as* *you enter town. Tel. 928-735-7514. Open 10am-5pm Memorial Day-Labor Day, Thursday -Sunday & Holidays. $2 Adult. $1 Youth 12-17.*

In the winter, skiers flock to nearby **Sunrise Park Resort** (*sunriseskiparkaz. com*) Their 65 runs off of ten lifts offer challenges for skiers of all levels, although the majority of the runs are beginner and intermediate. They also have a separate snowboarding area, cross-country ski trails, snow tubing, and a special children's "ski-wee" area. You can also ride the chair lift up for some great views in the summer.

## GREER
### Greer Peaks Lodge $-$$
This recently remodeled hotel is a good bet for family fun in Greer. The property amenities include whirlpools, a sauna, a fitness room and a game room. The comfortable rooms include flat screen TVs and the suites have fireplaces. Breakfast is complementary. *Info: www.greerpeakslodge.com. Tel. 928-735-9977. 1 Main Street.*

### X-Diamond Ranch $$
A working ranch since the early 1900s, the X-Diamond offers something for everybody. Horseback riding is one of the favorite activities, but you can also hike, fish, and even participate in an archeological dig on the ranch's own ruin site. Six large and comfortable cabins, within walking distance

### Gourmet Guest Ranch
For a guest ranch experience that includes gourmet meals and luxury accommodations, try **Hidden Meadow Ranch**. Depending on their capacity, they also accept some reservations for lunch, dinner, and Saturday brunch if you are staying elsewhere. The meal will be well-worth the trip if it fits in your budget. *Info: www.hiddenmeadow. com. Tel. 866-333-4080.*

of the Little Colorado River, are more like nice houses. Plenty of elk and deer roaming around through the pines. *Info: www.xdiamondranch.com. Tel. 928-333-2286. East of Greer off of AZ-260. 6 cabins.*

**Molly Butler Lodge $$-$**
In business since the early 1900s, the Molly Butler Lodge is a simple, rustic place that makes you feel right at home. The three lodge rooms are simple but comfortable. The Lodge also rents out over 50 cabins in the Greer area. The restaurant serves good country-style meals, while the lounge is a fun place to spend an evening shooting pool and feeding the juke box. *Info: www.mollybutlerlodge.com. Tel. 866-288-3167. 109 Main Street. 3 rooms.*

**Rendezvous Diner $**
Housed in what was once Greer's main post office, this diner is now a wonderful spot for home-cooking and tasty desserts. The small restaurant features friendly staff in a very informal atmosphere. Ask about pie specials and be sure to order them ala mode. *Info: Tel. 928-735-7483. 117 Main Street. Open daily breakfast, lunch and dinner.*

## PINETOP-LAKESIDE
Further west on AZ-260, **Pinetop-Lakeside** is the largest and most developed recreational center in the area. The summer population here can reach as high as 30,000 as desert dwellers from Phoenix seek higher ground. There are many lakes and an extensive trail system for hiking and biking. A highlight of this area is the **Mogollon Rim Overlook**, two miles northwest of town. An easy nature trail is marked with signs pointing out the abundant natural resources found in this area. The trail ends at the top of a sandstone rock outcrop with an outstanding view of the valley beneath the rim.

## WHERE TO STAY & EAT
### PINETOP-LAKESIDE
**Whispering Pines Resort $-$$**
Great location secluded in the pines on 12 acres of land bordering National Forest. The simple but comfortable cabins come in studio, one, two, and three and bedroom configurations. All come stocked with wood for the fireplace. There are paths to both Woodland Lake and Walnut Creek from the property. Quiet and peaceful yet also family friendly with a playground for kids. *Info: www.whisperingpinesaz.com. Tel. 800-840-3867. AZ-260, just beyond mile marker 352, Pinetop. 35 cabins.*

### Quality Inn Pinetop $

With clean, affordable rooms, this is a good option for those on a budget. All rooms come with refrigerators and breakfast is included. A very friendly staff makes for a pleasant experience. *Info: www.choicehotels.com/arizona/ pinetop/quality-inn-hotels/az089. Tel. 800-222-2244. 458 E. White Mountain Blvd, Pinetop. 42 rooms.*

### Charlie Clark's Steakhouse $$

A fun and casual place for a real western dinner. The building looks like a frontier cabin in the woods. Choose from a host of hearty fare that includes delicious slow cooked prime rib, rotisserie chicken, and mesquite steaks grilled to perfection. The atmosphere and food appeal to both children and adults. *Info: Tel. 928-367-4900. 1701 E White Mountain Blvd, Pinetop. Open nightly. Reservations recommended.*

### Red Devil Pizza $

Sometimes you want a break from "country-cooking" even when you are high in the pines. In that case, drive straight to Red Devil Pizza to get your fix of delicious pizza pie and other Italian yummies. It can get crowded on the weekends, so go before you are hungry. Take-out available. *Info: Tel. 928-367-5570. 1774 E White Mountain Blvd. Open daily 11am-9pm (10pm on Friday and Saturday).*

## PAYSON

The scenic drive along AZ-260 from Pinetop to **Payson** roughly parallels the Mogollon Rim. The road passes though a number of towns and recreational areas before a series of rather steep switchbacks brings you from the top of the rim into Payson, at the rim's base. Like Pinetop-Lakeside, Payson is a center for services related to the many recreational pursuits found in the White Mountains.

A highlight here is the **Tonto Natural Bridge State Park**. Composed of travertine, the bridge is 183 feet high while the space beneath it measures about 150 feet in height and almost 400 feet across. It is one of the largest natural structures of its type in the entire world and is visible from several viewpoints in the park. There is also a trail that leads from the top of bride into the canyon beneath. *Info: azstateparks.com/Parks/TONA. 10 miles north of Payson on AZ-87. Tel. 928-476-4202. 8am-6pm daily. $7 for adults, $4 youth 7-13.*

## WHERE TO STAY & EAT
### PAYSON
**Kohl's Ranch Lodge $$-$$$**
This delightful forest-surrounded lodge almost qualifies as a guest ranch.

Types of accommodations include motel-type bedrooms, multi-bedroom units, and several large cabins. Some include full kitchens. The recreational facilities are extensive and impressive — heated swimming pool, sauna, whirlpool, exercise room, sports court, horseshoes, bocce ball, and golf. There are hiking and jogging trails in the surrounding woods. Biking and horseback riding can also be arranged. *Info: www.kohlsranch.com. Tel. 800-521-3131. East Highway 260. 49 rooms.*

**Beeline Café $**
This small café seems like a throw-back to another decade. Nothing nouveau here, just good, stick-to-your-ribs comfort food. The hearty breakfasts are a real favorite, but any meal will give you a good taste of small-town living. Just don't be in a hurry. *Info: Tel. 928-747-9960. 815 S. Beeline Highway.*

## SHOPPING
### EASTERN ARIZONA
There are antique and craft shops to poke around in both Greer and Pinetop. Stores in Holbrook and Winslow carry some nice quality Native American-made goods.

## NIGHTLIFE & ENTERTAINMENT
### EASTERN ARIZONA
Some of the larger hotels in the region have live music during busy seasons, but in reality the nightlife in this area is pretty sparse. There are a number of casinos however, including the **Apache Gold Casino** outside of Globe (*www.apache-gold-casino.com, Tel. 800-272-2438*), the **Mazatzal Casino** in Payson (*www.mazatzal-casino.com, Tel. 800-777-7529*), the **Hon Dah Casino** outside of Pinetop (*www.hon-dah.com, Tel. 800-929-8744*).

## SPORTS & RECREATION
### EASTERN ARIZONA
#### Fishing
There are numerous lakes for fishing in the **White Mountains**. Try the Bunch, River, and Tunnel Lakes around Greer; Fred's Lake, 1/4 mile south of AZ 260 between Hon-Dah and Pinetop; or Rainbow Lake, off AZ 260 in Lakeside. The Little Colorado River in Greer is also a fisherman's delight.

#### Golf
There are plenty of public courses in the region. Try the **Alpine Country Club** (*Tel. 928-339-4944*) in Alpine; the **Payson Golf Course** (*Tel. 928-474-2273*) in Payson; or the **Pinetop Lakes Golf and Country Club** in Pinetop (*Tel. 928-369-4531*). The **Silver Creek Golf Club** near Show Low a Golf Digest 4-star course (*Tel. 928-537-2744*).

#### Hiking
Near Holbrook, the **Petrified Forest National Park** has a series of trails that wind through the incredible colored stone stumps.

In the White Mountains near Greer, you can climb **Mt. Baldy**, the second highest peak in the state, or **Escudilla Mountain**, the third highest, or just enjoy the intricate series of trails strewn throughout the **Apache-Sitgreaves National Forest** (*www.fs.usda.gov/activity/asnf/recreation/hiking*).

Hannagan Meadow abuts the **Blue Range Primitive Area**, where you can literally hike for days (*www.fs.usda.gov/recarea/asnf/recarea/?recid=75388*). Unfortunately this area was severely affected by the Wallow Fire in 2011 and is still in a phase of recovery.

Pinetop-Lakeside has the **White Mountains Trail System**, a series of 11 loop trails in the Lakeside Ranger District (*www.ci.pinetop-lakeside.az.us/trailsystem.htm*).

There are plenty of hikes around Payson as well. They range from the one-mile loop at the **Tonto Natural Bridge State Park** to the 51-mile **Highline Trail** (*www.arizonahikingtrails.com/paysonhikes.asp*).

#### Horseback Riding
If you want to explore the area on horseback, there are plenty of good options. In Greer call the **X Diamond Ranch** (*Tel. 928-333-2286*); in

Hannagan Meadow arrange ahead with the **Hannagan Meadow Stables** (*Tel. 928-339-4370*) and in the Pinetop-Lakeside area try **Porter Mountain Stables** (*Tel. 928-368-9599*).

### Skiing

**Sunrise Park Resort**, 15 minutes from Greer and 35 minutes from Pinetop-Lakeside, offers the most consistent snow in the state as they have well-developed snow-making facilities. With 65 runs, a terrain park for snowboarders, a snow tube area, a Ski-Wee area for the kids, and cross-country skiing, there is something for everyone (*www.sunriseskipark.com, Tel. 800-772-7669*).

# 8. WESTERN ARIZONA

**HIGHLIGHTS**

• **Hualapai Mountain**, near Kingman

• **Lake Havasu** and the real **London Bridge**

• A **trail ride** at one of Wickenburg's guest ranches

The western portion of Arizona is a land of wide-open spaces dotted by widely-spaced towns. This entire region is almost all **high desert**, which explains why its most important natural feature is the life-sustaining **Colorado River**. The river and its dams are the basis for numerous communities along its banks — like **Lake Havasu** and **Bullhead City/Laughlin** — which offer wet recreational pursuits and a party atmosphere in the middle of the desert. To the east of Kingman you'll find **Wickenburg**, one of the dude ranch capitals of the state.

## ORIENTATION

Lake Havasu is about 220 miles from Phoenix; take I-10 westbound to AZ 95. Wickenburg is less than an hour northwest of Phoenix via US 60. Kingman, along the old Route 66, is reached by I-40.

## KINGMAN

Tracing its beginnings to the coming of the railroad in 1880, Kingman is sustained by its important location on the interstate and its historic location on Route 66. The historic downtown area is centered around Beale Street. Start at the **Mohave Museum of History and Art**. The museum contains displays and several dioramas that trace the area history, including that of the Mohave and Hualapai Indian tribes. The most famous person to come out of Kingman is movie star Andy Devine. Another section of the museum houses a tribute to his television and movie star days. *Info: www. mohavemuseum.org, Tel. 928-753-3195. Monday-Friday 9am-5pm. Saturday 1pm-5pm. $2 adults. $1 children.*

Associated with and just down the street from the museum is the **Bonelli House**. Considered one of the best examples of the Anglo-territorial architectural style, it contains period pieces typical of a home of a prosperous Kingman family at the turn of the 20<sup>th</sup> century. A highlight is the large wall clock that, at one time, was the only clock in Kingman. *Info: www.mohavemuseum.org/bonel.html . 430 E Spring St. Tel. 928-753-3175. Monday-Friday 11am-3pm.*

Another good downtown stop is **Route 66 Museum**. The first paved transcontinental road in the country, Route 66 kept Kingman hopping in the '50s and '60s. The exhibits include old diners and period gas pumps. *Info: www.route66museum.net. 120 West Andy Devine Ave. in the Powerhouse Visitor's Center. Tel. 928-753-9889. Open 9am-6pm daily. $4 adults, $2 youth ages 8-18.*

**Around Kingman**

The old mining town of **Chloride** is a delightful day trip from Kingman. At one time more than 75 separate silver mines supported a population of over 2,000 people. Now the 300 residents, mostly artisans and craftsmen, have set up shop in some of the town's historic buildings. It's a fun place to spend a while poking around antique shops and galleries.

Continuing north, you'll reach the **Hoover Dam**, one of the great engineering wonders of the world. Seven hundred twenty six feet high, and completed in 1935, the dam is best visited early in the day before the throngs arrive from nearby Las Vegas. Several parking areas on the Arizona side provide a panoramic view of the top of the dam, with the brilliant azure blue of **Lake Mead** behind it and the dark Colorado River below. You can walk across to the Nevada side of the dam, where the visitor's center is located, for tours and more information. *Info: www.usbr.gov/lc/hooverdam. US93. Tel. 702-494-2517. 9am-5pm daily. $10 for visitor's center parking. Tours $15 adults, $12 children 7-16.*

Another worthwhile sight north of Kingman is the remote section of the Grand Canyon on the Hualapai Reservation called **Grand Canyon West**. This area features the famous glass **Skywalk**. A horseshoe shaped glass-bottomed overlook, the Skywalk juts 60 feet out over the rim of the canyon and hovers 3600 feet over the bottom. *Info: Tel. 877-716-9378. 80 miles northwest of Kingman. www.grandcanyonwest.com. $72 per person to see and walk on bridge (see end of Grand Canyon chapter).*

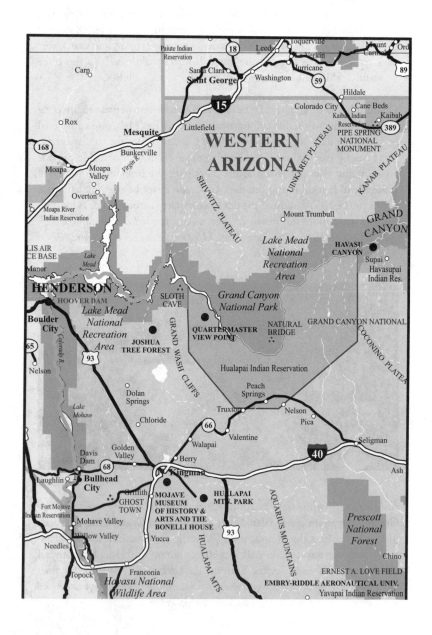

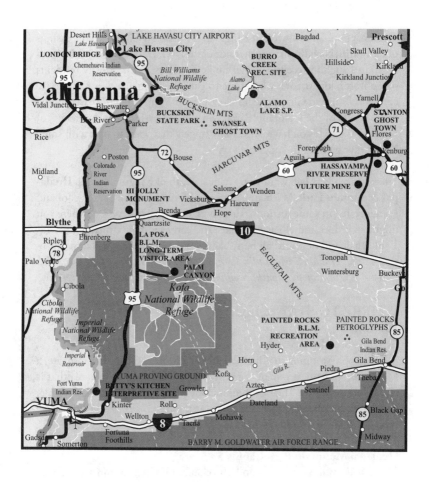

Desert Hills
Lake Havasu
LONDON BRIDGE
Chemehuevi Indian
Reservation
LAKE HAVASU CITY AIRPORT
Lake Havasu City
95
Bill Williams
National Wildlife
Refuge
Alamo
Lake
Bagdad
Prescott
Skull Valley
Hillside
Kirkland
Kirkland Junction
BURRO
CREEK
REC. SITE

California
95
Vidal Junction
Bluewater
Big River
Parker
BUCKSKIN MTS
BUCKSKIN
STATE PARK
SWANSEA
GHOST TOWN
ALAMO
LAKE S.P.
Yarnell
Congress
STANTON
GHOST
TOWN
Flores
71

Rice
Poston
Colorado
River
Indian
Reservation
72
Bouse
HARCUVAR MTS
Forepaugh
Aguila
Wickenburg
60

Midland
95
HI JOLLY
MONUMENT
Vicksburg
Salome
Harcuvar
Wenden
HASSAYAMPA
RIVER PRESERVE
VULTURE MINE
60

Blythe
Ripley
Ehrenberg
Brenda
Hope
Quartzsite
LA POSA
B.L.M.
LONG-TERM
VISITOR AREA
PALM
CANYON
10

Palo Verde
78
Cibola
Cibola
National Wildlife
Refuge
Imperial
National Wildlife
Refuge
95
Kofa
National Wildlife
Refuge
EAGLETAIL MTS.
Tonopah
Wintersburg
Buckeye
Go

Imperial
Reservoir
PAINTED ROCKS
B.L.M.
RECREATION
AREA
Hyder
PAINTED ROCKS
PETROGLYPHS
Gila Bend
Indian Res.
85

Fort Yuma
Indian Res.
YUMA
BETTY'S KITCHEN
INTERPRETIVE SITE
Kinter
YUMA PROVING GROUND
Kofa
Growler
Horn
Gila R.
Aztec
Piedra
Sentinel
Gila Bend
Theba
85
Black Gap

Gadsden
Somerton
Wellton
Fortuna
Foothills
Roll
8
Taena
Mohawk
Dateland
BARRY M. GOLDWATER AIR FORCE RANGE
Midway

East of Kingman you'll find the delightfully cool **Grand Canyon Caverns.** You can see colorful formations and marine fossils dating back more than three million years as well as evidence of visitation by Native Americans. Guided tours begin with a 21-story elevator descent into the 56-degree cavern. The tour, on well-lit paved trails, lasts about 45 minutes. *Info: www. gccaverns.com. East of Kingman on AZ-66. Tel. 928-422-3223. 10am-4pm daily (8am-6pm in summer.) $17 adults. $13 children 4-12.*

The most popular spot west of Kingman is **Bullhead City**, with the casinos of **Laughlin, Nevada** on the other side of the river. Despite its rather isolated location Laughlin receives several million visitors a year, mostly residents of California or Arizona who come to gamble. Regular water taxi service connects Bullhead City to the hotel-casinos lined up along the banks of the Nevada side of the Colorado River. Most of the casinos are "branches" of those in Vegas. If you have some itchy fingers that want to part with some bucks, give gaming in Laughlin a try.

Hikers and bikers will want to travel just south of Kingman to the **Hualapai Mountain Park**. With an elevation of 8400 feet, the park is cool and even forested in some sections. There is an extensive trail system where you might spot deer and elk as you hike. You can even rent a picnic kit, with a volleyball and net, softball bats, balls and bases, a soccer ball and horseshoes. *Info: Hualapai Mountain Park, 6230 Hualapai Mountain Road. Tel. 928-681-5700. www.mcparks.com/hualapai_mt_park.htm. $7 per vehicle.*

## WHERE TO STAY & EAT
### KINGMAN
### El Trovatore Motel $
Many people stopping in Kingman are on a Route 66 trip. El Travatore, a Mother Road icon, is one of the only pre-WWII hotels in the area that is still a working motel. Theme rooms include Marylyn Monroe, Clark Gable, and James Deans, who were all guests at the hotel. *Info: eltrovatoremotel. com. Tel. 928-753-6520. 1440 E. Andy Devine Ave.*

### Hualapai Mountain Park Cabins $
These rustic cabins offer the wonderful chance for a high-mountain getaway very near Kingman. Some come with fireplaces or wood burning stoves. You must bring your own bedding materials. *Info: www.mcparks.com/ hmp_rv_and_resort_accommodations.html. Hualapai Mountain Park, 6230 Hualapai Mountain Road. Tel. 928-757-0915.*

**Hualapai Mountain Resort $-$$**
To call this property a resort might be stretching things, but that doesn't diminish the appeal of this woodsy mountain getaway only 20 minutes from downtown Kingman. Surrounded by granite-studded mountains and ponderosa pines, the resort offers 6 rooms, dining and a bar. The newly remodeled rooms, decorated with lodge-style touches, are quite comfortable and some include fireplaces. Elk are deer are often spotted on the grounds. The restaurant is surprisingly good, with hearty dishes and homemade pastries. *Info: www.hmresort.net. Tel. 928-757-3545. 4525 Hualapai Mountain Road. 6 rooms.*

**Dambar & Steakhouse $-$$**
Although thick and juicy steaks are the main attraction at Dambar, the menu has a wide variety of items including sandwiches and salads. Friendly and efficient service. Popular with locals, so you might have to wait a bit on weekends. *Info: Tel. 928-753-3523. 1960 E. Andy Devine. Lunch and dinner daily.*

**Hualapai Mountain Resort Dining Room $-$$**
Located up the road from Kingman in the Hualapai Mountains, this restaurant is worth the drive. Not only will you experience a complete change of scenery, you'll enjoy delicious, hearty, home-style dishes like ribs, steak, and grilled chicken accompanied with warm home-made bread. Save room for the cobbler for dessert. Live music on weekends. Reservations recommended. *Info: Tel. 928-757-3545. 4525 Hualapai Mountain Road. Open for breakfast, lunch, and dinner daily.*

## NIGHTLIFE & ENTERTAINMENT
### BULLHEAD CITY/LAUGHLIN
People come here to gamble. In Laughlin you can find Vegas-imported casinos such as the **Golden Nugget** and **Harrah's**, and local places like the **Aquarius**. Or, for that whole Mississippi River vibe, try the **Colorado Belle**. All are located on the Nevada side of the Colorado River, which is Laughlin's "strip" if you will.

## LAKE HAVASU CITY
One of Arizona's popular "west coast" resort destinations, **Lake Havasu City** sits on the east side of the lake of the same name. It's a beautiful lake destination – complete with the real London Bridge of song – but the appeal for many visitors is the non-stop party scene.

The **London Bridge** survived many historic events in England, but could not withstand nature's forces. In 1968, the city of London decided to sell the sinking bridge for 2.5 million dollars to Robert P. McCulloch, founder of Lake Havasu City. Transported brick-by-brick from its original Thames River location, the bridge was rebuilt across a small man-made channel of the Colorado River. The bridge is open at all times and illuminated at night.

An **English village** has grown up around the bridge, offering shopping, restaurants, and the biggest night club in the southwest. **Bridgewater Channel**, which the bridge spans, is the hub of the party scene in Lake Havasu City. During the day boats tie up side-to-side along the channel with radios blasting and beer flowing. In the evening the party moves to the channel's edge at the **Heat Hotel** and **Kokomo night club**.

The surrounding resort area covers 110 acres and features all sorts of recreation opportunities, lake cruises, and a marina. A walking path spans both sides of Bridgewater Channel. Both ends of the path are anchored by city parks. **London Bridge Park** includes a large beach, volleyball courts, and children's play areas. You can rent any kind of boat or personal watercraft and enjoy the almost always sunny weather. The lake and river can be seen best by boat tours. Try **Blue Water Jet Boat** tours for a two-hour trip up the Colorado River (*Tel. 888-855-717. www.coloradoriverjetboattours.com*). **Western Arizona Canoe**

**& Kayak Outfitters** is a good option if you prefer to travel under your own steam. (*Tel. 888-881-5038. www.azwacko.com*).

The excellent **Havasu National Wildlife Refuge** is located just to the north, in scenic Topock Gorge. It can be seen by either boat or foot trail. Geese, egrets, and heron are big attractions to birders. *Info: Tel. 760-326-3853. www.fws.gov/refuge/Havasu. 7:30am-3:30pm daily. Free entry.*

## WHERE TO STAY & EAT
### LAKE HAVASU
**London Bridge Resort $$-$$$**

A most attractive waterfront resort, it is part of the complex that contains the London Bridge and the shopping village. The rooms are actually studio, one bedroom, and two bedroom suites. Some have excellent lake views. Recreational facilities include swimming pools, spa, tennis, and golf as well as every water sport imaginable. Private sandy beach. Two restaurants and a cocktail lounge. *Info: Tel. 866-331-9231. www.londonbridgeresort.com. In the center of town on Thompson Bay. 1477 Queen's Bay Road. 122 suites.*

**Heat Hotel $$-$$$**
This hip, modern hotel is at the epicenter of Lake Havasu party-life. Located on Bridgewater Channel at the foot of the London Bridge, all you have to do is step out your door for the party to begin. The hotel is conveniently located within walking distance of beaches, restaurants, and foot paths. The rooms and suites are very sleek with modern furniture, flat screen TVs and Ipod hook-ups. The Tempur-Pedic beds are divine, as are the large, jetted tubs. Both the hotel's Patio Bar and the nightclub across the channel blast music late into the night on weekends, but it's not an issue if you are out partying anyway. Things are calmer on weekdays, with the exception of Spring Break. *Info: www.heathotel.com. Tel. 888-898-4328. 1420 McCullough Blvd.*

### Sands Vacation Resort $-$$

Another all-suite facility featuring either one or two bedroom apartments with full kitchens. The suites are spacious and comfortable with a separate living area. Heated pool, tennis court, horseshoes, and bocce. *Info: Tel. 800-521-0360. www.havasusands.com. One mile from bridge at 2040 Mesquite Ave. 42 suites.*

### Martini Bay Lounge & Restaurant $$

Located inside the London Bridge Resort, Martini Bay has excellent outdoor seating on multiple verandas and patios. Specializing in tapas, little dishes from Spain that are meant to be ordered by the plateful and shared, Martini Bay has created a fun atmosphere and serves good food. Martinis, of course, are the house specialty. *Info: Tel. 928-855-0888. www.londonbridgeresort. com. In the center of town on Thompson Bay. 1477 Queen's Bay Road. Dinner served Tuesday-Saturday starting at 4pm.*

### Shugrue's $$-$$$

Enjoy upscale dining overlooking London Bridge. Menu items include Prime Rib, steaks, seafood specialties, and pasta dishes. Lots of diners come for special events like anniversaries and birthdays. *Info: Tel. 928-453-1400. 1425 McCullough Blvd. Reservations recommended.*

### Javelina Cantina $-$$

With its central location at one end of the London Bridge, Javelina Cantina is a popular spot for boaters and land-based visitors alike. With both indoor and outdoor seating, you can either escape or bask in the sun at this fun Mexican eatery. If you don't come hungry, you may want to split a meal, as the plates are huge. The margaritas are large and powerful. *Info: Tel. 928-855-8226. 1420 McCullough Blvd. Reservations recommended on weekends.*

### Mudshark Brewing Company $-$$

With great pizza and burgers, friendly service, and tasty beers to sample, the Mudshark is a favorite for locals and visitors alike. Try the Scorpion Amber Ale with the Mushroom Swiss Burger and you'll go home happy for sure. *Info: Tel. 928-453-2981. 210 Swanson Ave. Open for lunch and dinner daily.*

## SHOPPING
### LAKE HAVASU

The **English Village** at the foot of the London Bridge is the place for shopping. There are over 40 stores located here.

## NIGHTLIFE & ENTERTAINMENT
### LAKE HAVASU

The nightlife in Lake Havasu can be found in the lounges and bars along the waterfront and in the London Bridge area. Two good bets are **Kokomo's** on (*Queen's Bay Road, Tel. 928-855-8782*) or **Flying X Cantina**, *2030 McCulloch Blvd N, Tel. 928-854-3599*. For cool drinks in a great location overlooking Bridgewater Channel, try the outdoor bar at the **Heat Hotel**, *1420 McCullough Blvd. Tel. 888-898-4328*. The **Engish Village**, mentioned above, also has restaurants, entertainment and activities.

## SPORTS & RECREATION
### LAKE HAVASU

People come to Lake Havasu to enjoy the lake. Boat tours are a very popular option. Try **Blue Water Jet Boat Tours** for a two-hour trip up the Colorado River (*Tel. 888-855-717, www.coloradoriverjetboattours.com*). **Western Arizona Canoe & Kayak Outfitters** rents all sorts of self-propelled watercraft (*Tel. 888-881-5038, www.azwacko.com*).

Even if you don't have a watercraft, you can enjoy the lake at one of the city's public beaches. Try **London Bridge Beach**, on the island across from London Bridge; **Rotary Beach Park**, south of the bridge; or **Lake Havasu State Park** north of the bridge.

For golf, try the **London Bridge Golf Club** (*Tel. 928-855-2719*) with two 18-hole championship courses; or the 9-hole executive course at the **London Bridge Resort** (Tel. 928-855-4777).

## YUMA

Despite being one of the hottest locations in the United States, it is the weather in **Yuma** that attracts so many visitors. Comfortable winters, low humidity, and sunshine a staggering 93% of the time, make Yuma ideal for every sun worshipper.

Start your day at the **Yuma Territorial Prison State Park**, situated on a high bluff overlooking the Colorado River. A maximum security prison from 1876-1909, when Arizona really was the Wild West, it can now be toured on your own or with a guide. Don't miss the solitary confinement area known as "the hole." *Info: 1 Prison Hill Road. Tel. 928-783-4771. azstateparks.com/parks/yute. 8am-5pm daily. $6 adults. $3 children.*

Nearby on 2nd Avenue on a site by the Colorado River that also faces Yuma's city hall is the **Yuma Quartermaster Depot State Historic Park**. A Quartermaster Depot was established here in 1865 to serve as a major storage and distribution point for supplies. Guides costumed in period clothing are on hand to relate the tales and history of the site. Also located here is a Southern Pacific steam locomotive. *Info: 201 N. 4th Avenue. Tel. 928-329-0471. azstateparks.com/Parks/YUQU. 9am-5pm daily. $4 adults. $2 children.*

A final downtown stop is the **Sanguinetti House Museum.** The former home of a wealthy Yuma merchant, the house now exhibits furnishings and artifacts representative of Yuma's frontier period. The original owner had a colorful garden with bird aviaries and these are also maintained as they were in the past. The talking birds are sure to delight children. *Info: 240 Madison Avenue. Tel. 928-782-1841. www.yumalibrary.org/ahs. Monday-Friday 10am-3pm. $6 ages 13 and over.*

### Nice Stop in Yuma

Try the **Garden Café**, behind the Sanguinetti House, for a nice breakfast or lunch in the inviting tree-shaded garden. Leave room for dessert. *Info: 250 Madison Ave. Tel. 928-783-1491.*

## WHERE TO STAY & EAT
### YUMA
### La Fuente Inn & Suites $-$$

With spacious and attractive grounds, La Fuente is an oasis in the desert. The building's architecture is Spanish style and the front entrance features a large fountain with water tumbling down a series of boulders. The inner courtyard has well manicured lawns bordered by trees and shrubs that enclose the swimming pool and pretty gazebo. The rooms are simply but thought-

fully furnished. Facilities include a heated pool, whirlpool, and exercise room. There is no restaurant, but a continental breakfast is included as are evening complimentary beverages. *Info: www.lafuenteinn.com. Tel. 800-841-1814. 1513 East 16$^{th}$ St. 96 rooms.*

### El Pappagallo Mexican Restaurant $-$$

Great Mexican food served by very nice people. Try the huevos rancheros or carne asada. The salsa is made fresh daily. *Info: Tel. 928-343-9451. 1401 S Avenue B. Open daily 11am-9pm.*

# WICKENBURG

Tracing its origins to prospector Henry Wickenburg, the town of **Wickenburg** was once an important center for **gold, copper and silver mining**. It prospers now because of its great weather and dude ranches. Visit one of the state's guest ranches if you get the chance. Wickenburg has three that are members of the reputable **Arizona Dude Ranch Association** (*www. azdra.com*). Some guest ranches are true working ranches and others are ranch vacation destinations – be sure to decide which you want before you make reservations.

**Rancho de los Caballeros** is a great option for families with varied interests and priorities. As one of the largest and nicest guest ranches in Arizona,

it offers many amenities that other ranches can't match, including a championship golf course and pampering spa. There is also a heated pool as well as morning and evening children's programs, which means that the kids have a ball even when they are not riding horses.

The "formal" dinners (jackets or vests are required for men) are tasty and wonderfully civilized. Beautiful location in the mountains of the Sonoran Desert. *Info: 1551 S. Vulture Mine Road. Tel. 800-684-5030. www.sunc. com. 79 rooms. Open October-May.*

Riding is the focus at the **Flying E Ranch**. While non-riders can enjoy the heated pool, tennis, and shuffleboard, it's the horseback riders who rave about this place. With a capacity of 34 guests, this working ranch is small enough to offer personalized riding sessions. The home-style meals are nice and hearty. There is no bar, but you can bring your own liquor and they provide the ice. *Info: 2801 W. Wickenburg Way. Tel. 928-684-2690. www. flyingeranch.com. 14 rooms, 3 suites.*

The **Desert Caballeros Western Museum** features special exhibits that change often and are usually quite good, but it's the permanent collection that really tells the story of the West. Artists displayed include big guns like Frederick Remington and Charles Russell. The wonderful Spirit of the Cowboy collection showcases finely wrought saddles, boots, bridles and chaps that are truly works of art. There's even a replica of 1915 Wickenberg complete with a saloon. *Info: 21 N Frontier St. Tel. 928-684-2272. www. westernmuseum.org. 10 am–5pm daily. (12pm-4pm Sunday). $12 adults. Free children 17 and under.*

# WHERE TO STAY & EAT
## WICKENBURG
The best places to stay in Wickenburg are the area's outstanding **guest ranches** (see above). If you make your way into town from one of the ranches, however, and want to grab a bite while you are there, check out the following restaurants:

### Horseshoe Café $
For classic café food right off the grill, this is the place to stop. Breakfast favorites like biscuits and gravy and hash browns are served through lunch time, along with burgers, patty melts, and grilled Reubens. This place has been around for 50 years and, based on the breakfast and lunch crowd, will keep going strong for years to come. *Info: Tel. 928-684-7377. 207 E Wickenburg Way. Open daily breakfast and lunch.*

### Nana's Sandwich Saloon $
This fun little restaurant serves up a rotating menu of quiches, sandwiches,

soups, and dessert all made with excellent, high quality ingredients. *Info: Tel. 928-684-5539. 48 N. Tagner St. Open from breakfast through lunch Monday-Saturday.*

## SHOPPING
### WICKENBURG
Pick up the perfect western outfit at **Double D Western Wear**, *955 W. Wickenburg Way, Tel. 928-684-7987*. North Tenger and Frontier streets also have a number of western wear stores as well as small shops and galleries.

## SPORTS & RECREATION
### WICKENBURG
Most people come to Wickenburg for the dude ranches, so obviously **horseback riding** is a popular option here. Day visitors who aren't staying at a dude ranch can rent horses at **Polly Anne's Wickenburg Stables**, *Tel. 928-684-7331.*

Golfers can hit the links at the **Los Caballeros Golf Club**, which is part of the Los Caballeros dude ranch (*Tel. 928-684-2704, www.sunc.com/golf.html*).

**BC Jeep Tours** (*Tel. 928-684-7901, www.bcjeeptours.com*) is another fun way to see the countryside.

# 10. PRACTICAL MATTERS

## GETTING TO ARIZONA
### Airports & Arrivals
Arizona's busiest airport and the one with the greatest choice of airlines and flights is Phoenix's **Sky Harbor International Airport**. However, if you're going to be concentrating on the southern part of the state the airport in Tucson is a good secondary choice.

Two major airlines have an important presence at Phoenix Sky Harbor. These are **American Airlines** and discount maverick **Southwest Airlines**. Both of them have more non-stop destinations from Phoenix than any other airlines. Check them first.

These are the main carriers serving Phoenix:

* **Air Canada**, *Tel. 888/247-2262, www.aircanada.com*
* **Alaska Airlines**, *Tel. 800/426-0333, www.alaskaair.com*
* **American**, *Tel. 800/433-7300, www.aa.com*
* **British Airways**, *Tel. 800/247-9297, www.britishairway.com*
* **Delta Airlines**, *Tel. 800/221-1212, www.delta.com*
* **Frontier Airlines**, *Tel. 800/432-1359, www.flyfrontier.com*
* **Great Lakes Airlines**, *Tel. 554-5111, www.greatlakesav.com*
* **Hawaiian Airlines**, *Tel. 800/367-5320, www.hawaiianair.com*
* **JetBlue Airways**, *Tel. 800/538-2583, www.jetblue.com*
* **Southwest Airlines**, *Tel. 800/435-9792, www.southwest.com*
* **Spirit Airlines**, *Tel. 801/401-2222, www.spirit.com*
* **Sun Country Airlines**, *Tel. 800/359-6786, www.suncountry.com*
* **United Airlines**, *Tel. 800/241-6522, www.ual.com*
* **Volaris Airlines**, *Tel. 855/865-2747, www.volaris.com.mx*
* **West Jet Airlines**, *Tel. 888/937-8538, www.westjet.com*

Phoenix Sky Harbor is host to many international flights on both domestic and foreign airlines.

Another airport in the greater Phoenix area is the **Phoenix-Mesa Gateway Airport**, which currently only handles **Allegiant Air** flights, but covers many different destinations. (*www.allegiantair.com, Tel. 702-505-8888.*)

**Tucson International Airport** is much smaller and handles far fewer flights, although a number of the same airlines that serve Phoenix can also take you to Tucson. They are Alaska, American, Delta, Southwest, and United.

Both the Phoenix and Tucson airports offer straightforward arrivals to the city. There are cabs, shuttle services, hotel courtesy vans, and city buses at curbside as you exit the baggage claim area. The Phoenix airport has one central terminal for all car rentals that is accessed by a curbside bus. In Tucson the car rental companies have cars in a garage adjacent to the main terminal.

**Flagstaff Pulliam Airport** is small, but does offer direct flights to Phoenix on American Airlines. The Prescott Airport currently offers flights on Great Lakes Airlines to Los Angeles, Denver, Moab, Kingman, and Page.

## GETTING AROUND
### By Air
Both **American** and **United** have flights to cities within the state. **Scenic Airlines**, *Tel. 800/634-6801, www.scenic.com*, isn't so much a carrier as it is a tour operator. Their base is in Las Vegas and they offer day and overnight trips to both the Grand Canyon and Monument Valley in Arizona.

### By Car & Car Rental
A car, whether it's your own or a rental, is definitely the best way to get around in Arizona. Besides being the most time and cost effective method, it also offers the traveler a degree of flexibility that cannot be matched by any form of public transportation. If you from another country and plan to rent a car, be sure to have a valid International Drivers License. Here are the major car rental agencies with their phone numbrets in Phoenix followed by Tucson:

- **Alamo**, *www.alamo.com*
  *800/462-5266     602/244-0897     520/573-4740*
- **Avis**, *www.avis.com*
  *800/230-4898     602/273-3222     520/294-1494*
- **Budget**, *www.budget.com*
  *800/527-0700     602/267-1717     520/889-8800*

• **Dollar**, *www.dollar.com*
*800/800-3665     602/275-7588     520/573-8486*
• **Enterprise**, *www.enterprise.com*
*800/325-8007     602/225-0588     520/295-1964*
• **Hertz**, *www.hertz.com*
*800/654-3131     602/267-8822     520/294-7616*
• **National**, *www.nationalcar.com*
*800/227-7368     602/275-4771     520/573-8050*
• **Thrifty**, *www.thrifty.com*
*800/847-4389     602/244-0311     520/790-2277*

**Good driving maps of Arizona are available from AAA and major bookstores. The map put out by** the Office of Tourism is also an acceptable source. If you wait until your arrival in Arizona, you can purchase road maps at the Phoenix and Tucson airports.

### By Train
Like most of the western and mountain states, Arizona caters to the car driver. For those willing to put up with the inconvenience of public trans portation, here's some guidance on getting around from one city to another by train.

**Amtrak** serves a number of Arizona communities. The daily Southwest Chief (Chicago to Los Angeles) traverses the north-central portion of the state from east to west and has stops at Winslow, Flagstaff, and Kingman. Connecting bus service from Flagstaff is available to both the Grand Canyon and Phoenix. In the south, two separate trains serve Benson, Tucson, Maricopa, and Yuma. Each of these trains, the Sunset Limited (Florida to Los Angeles) and the Texas Eagle (Chicago to Los Angeles), runs three times a week. From Tucson there is connecting bus service to Phoenix. *Info: Tel. 800-USA-RAIL; www.amtrak.com.*

The state does have two excellent "tourist" train trips:

The **Grand Canyon Railway**: Passengers ride in carefully restored coaches that recreate the atmosphere of 1901 when service to the Grand Canyon was inaugurated. Vintage locomotives add to the authenticity of the 2-1/4 hour trip from Williams to the South Rim. You'll arrive at a depot that was built in 1910 and is the only log railroad station still in use in the nation. Visitors have about 3-1/2 hours of sightseeing time along the South Rim before the train returns to Williams, which is accessible from Phoenix via bus. *Info*: www.thetrain.com, Tel. 800-843-8724.

**Verde Canyon Railway**: The Verde Canyon Railway travels through a scenic portion of the Verde Canyon and Sycamore Wilderness that cannot be reached by road. The trip departs from Clarkdale, which is only a few miles from Sedona. The four-hour journey offers thrilling trestles that span deep canyons as well as views of ancient Indian ruins. Bus service is available to Sedona. You need a car or taxi to get to Clarkdale. *Info: www. verdecanyonrr.com, 800-320-0718.*

### By Taxi
Although Phoenix and Tucson are large, cosmopolitan cities, you won't be able to hail a cab on the street except for at the airport. You'll have to have your hotel call one for you. In smaller cities, the cab service is even spottier, although it does exist in medium-sized towns like Flagstaff and Sedona.

### By Ride Sharing
Both **Uber** and **Lyft** service the major cities in Arizona. They are easy to hail and much cheaper than cabs. You can download the apps in your smart phone's app store.

### By Bus
Bus service is provided by **Greyhound**. *Info*: *Tel. 800/231-2222 (for route Information and reservations), www.greyhound.com.*

Within the **Navajo Indian Reservation** there is regularly scheduled bus service along several different routes. This low-cost service is provided by the **Navajo Transit System**. They have 17 routes serving all of the region's major communities. *Info: www.navajotransit.com . Tel. 928/729-4002.*

## BASIC INFORMATION

### Business Hours

As is the case in much of the US, businesses are staying open later and later to accommodate busy schedules. Banks and government offices are generally still only open from 9-5. Museums often have one night a week that they stay open later than usual.

### Climate & Weather

Many people have the mistaken impression that Arizona is hot and dry all the time from one corner of the state to another. But, like everything else you'll encounter here, variation is the name of the game. Yes, many parts of the state have blistering arid summers and mild dry winters. However, winter is a very literal term for northern Arizona where heavy snow provides great skiing near Flagstaff and closes roads to the North Rim of the Grand Canyon for several months of the year. Therefore, the best time to visit Arizona depends upon what areas of the state you're going to be concentrating on and what outdoor activities you're planning.

### Temperature & Rainfall Averages
Temperature Highs/Lows & Annual Precipitation

|  | Jan. | April | July | Oct. | Precip. |
|---|---|---|---|---|---|
| Flagstaff | 41/14 | 57/27 | 81/50 | 63/31 | 19.8" |
| Grand Canyon | 41/17 | 59/30 | 83/52 | 64/34 | 13.1" |
| Kingman | 57/31 | 75/42 | 97/67 | 79/47 | 10.7" |
| Page | 45/23 | 67/38 | 94/63 | 71/42 | 10.2" |
| Phoenix | 65/38 | 84/52 | 105/77 | 88/57 | 7.0" |
| Prescott | 51/23 | 69/38 | 91/61 | 74/42 | 15.4" |
| Tucson | 63/38 | 81/50 | 98/74 | 84/56 | 11.0" |
| Yuma | 68/43 | 86/57 | 106/81 | 90/62 | 3.2" |

The northern portion of the state, roughly corresponding to the Colorado Plateau region, has mild to warm summers and cold winters. Precipitation comes mostly in the form of summertime thundershowers and some significant winter snowstorms. If you plan to spend all or most of your Arizona vacation in the north, the months from May through September are best.

The remainder of the state is mostly dry and hot in the summer. Temperatures in the desert sizzle during the day, especially in the **Phoenix** area and along the western edge of the state around Yuma. **Tucson** is a few degrees cooler and even that small variance can make quite a difference in comfort levels.

For a sightseeing vacation, the fall through winter is a better time to visit than the middle of summer. However, if you're coming to Arizona mainly to stay at a resort and sit by the pool, keep in mind that desert winters aren't like those in Florida – the heart of winter is often too cool to fully enjoy those types of activitie

A vacation that cuts across all parts of the state is also well suited to the less extreme weather conditions present in the fall or spring. However, it's probably much wiser to contend with the summer heat than risk not being able to get somewhere in the winter because of a heavy snow.

### Electricity
AC, 110 volts/60 cycles.

### Emergencies & Safety
In any emergency situation you should dial **911 for** coordinated assistance. All of Arizona is on this system and your call will be automatically routed to the nearest emergency service.

Safety concerns are no greater or less here than other parts of the country. Don't leave items lying around exposed in your car, even for a short time, and use lockboxes at hotels for valuables.

### Festivals & Holidays
Arizona observes all national holidays. Notable events include the **Rodeo Parade** in Tucson in February; **Cinco de Mayo** events around the state in May; **Frontier Days** in Prescott in June; **Independence Day** celebrations around the state in July; the **Coconino Country Fair** in Flagstaff in August; the **Navajo Nation Fair** in Window Rock in September; the **Arizona State Fair** in Phoenix in October; and **Christmas** lights and festivities all over the state in December.

### Telephones/Area Codes

Greater Phoenix has three area codes – 602 for the Central Valley, 480 for the East Valley, and 623 for the West Valley. Tucson and cities south are in area code 520. North of Phoenix is all 928.

You might want to keep in mind that most of Arizona, outside the Navajo Nation, does not observe daylight savings time. So, even if you are calling within the 928 area code, you might be calling to another time zone.

### Time

Although all of Arizona is on Mountain Time (two hours earlier than the east coast and one hour later than the west coast), things get complicated for two reasons. First of all, Arizona is one of the few states in the country that does not observe Daylight Savings Time. As a result, when most places are observing Daylight Savings Time, Arizona isn't, making it the same as Pacific Time. BUT, the Navajo Nation does observe Daylight Savings Time. So, when you are going somewhere like Monument Valley or Canyon del Chelly during the summer, it will be a different time there than it is in the rest of Arizona.

### Tipping

It is standard to tip 15-20% at restaurants on the total bill for meals (before tax), 10% for taxis, and $1-2 a day for maid service. And of course, if people provide exceptionally good service or go out of their way for you, a more generous tip is often given. Keep in mind that most people who are employed in the tourist industry, specifically hotels and restaurants, don't get great salaries. They count on tips for a significant part of their income.

### Tourist Information

The **Arizona Office of Tourism** (*www.visitarizona.com*) can supply you with a general state visitor's guide as well as numerous other brochures, special publications and maps. If you don't have access to the internet, you can call their **toll-free telephone information line** (*Tel. 888-520-3434 or 602-230-7733*). More specific information on cities and regions is available from local chambers of commerce or visitor bureaus.

### Websites

There are hundreds of internet sites devoted either exclusively or partially to Arizona and traveling in the state. Some of the more important statewide sites are listed here. Many localities have their own site as well.

**www.visitarizona.com**: This is the official website of the Arizona Office of Tourism and an extensive one with statewide information and many links.

**www.recreation.gov**: Covers areas managed by all federal agencies including the all-important National Parks Service.

**www.az.gov**: Official site of Arizona's state government. It has information on all aspects of Arizona, including tourism and lodging reservations.

# INDEX

## Photo Credits

pp. 155, p. 167 bottom: Rancho de los Caballeros

From Flickr: p. 9: Michael Chrobak; pp. 13, 105, 108: Wolfgang Staudt; pp. 14, 110, 111, p. 114 bottom 115, 121, 122: Grand Canyon NPS; p. 15: Keith Evans; p. 27: John Fowler; p. 29: Onasill ~ Bill Badzo; p. 43: Ben Cane; p. 45: Kevin.Cochran; pp. 46, 142: Bill Morrow; p. 51: b d; p. 54: contemplicity; p. 55: Dave Bezaire & Susi Havens-Bezaire; p. 56: Karen; p. 58: dlbezaire; p. 65: dennyforrea; p. 73: laszlo-photo; p. 74: John-Morgan; pp. 77, 93: Coconino National Forest; p. 79: meglet127; p. 84: CodyR; p. 86: edwindavila; p. 87 top: donds; p. 87 bottom: justincb123; p. 88: xinem; p. 96: sfbaywalk; p. 104: TaQpets; p. 114 top: hastin_m; pp. 118, 133: Ron Cogswell; p. 123: Reannon Muth; p. 124: Richard Martin; p. 128: Rennett Stowe; p. 130: Alan Vernon; p. 135, 138: Moyan_Brenn; p. 137: mark byzewski; p. 140: Philms; p. 141: Petrified Forest; p. 144: Paul Fundenburg; p. 148: sean hobson; p. 154: TLPOSCHARSKY; p. 157: rcgtrrz; p. 162: Graeme Maclean; p. 165: ~Pawsitive~Candie_N; p.169: irina slutsky; p. 177: puliarf.

# TRAVEL NOTES